THE ANNUAL REVIEW OF
W O M E N
IN
WORLD RELIGIONS
VOLUME II
HEROIC WOMEN

A book entitled: *Women in World Religions* was published by the SUNY Press in 1987. The reception indicated that it met a felt need. It also seemed to vindicate the historical and phenomenological approach to the study of women in world religions. The relevance of both subject and method seemed to call for an ongoing forum to contine discussing themes covered in the book. We therefore decided, with the cooperation of the SUNY Press, to launch a journal providing such a forum.

This journal will appear as an annual. Due to the common ground it shares with the book mentioned above, of which it is a lineal descendant, we have decided to call it *The Annual Review of Women in World Religions*.

This *Annual Review of Women in World Religions* has been conceived as polymethodic, interdisciplinary and multitraditional in its approach to the study of women and religion. It will not only allow the comparative dimension to appear in bolder relief, but will also help establish a dialogue between the two solitudes of humanistic and social scientific studies in the field. We hope that it will be welcomed in academic circles.

THE ANNUAL REVIEW OF
W O M E N
IN
WORLD RELIGIONS
VOLUME II
HEROIC WOMEN

Edited by
Arvind Sharma
and
Katherine K. Young

State University of New York Press

Published by
State University of New York Press, Albany

© 1992 State University of New York

For information, address State University of New York Press,
State University Plaza, Albany, N.Y. 12246

Production by Marilyn Semerad
Marketing by Lynne Lekakis

The Annual review of women in world religions
ISSN 1056-4578

ISBN 0-7914-1611-9

ISBN 0-7914-1612-7 (pbk.)

10   9   8   7   6   5   4   3   2   1

THE ANNUAL REVIEW OF WOMEN IN WORLD RELIGIONS

EXECUTIVE EDITORS

Arvind Sharma   Katherine K. Young

EDITORIAL BOARD

CONTENTS

HEROIC MODES OF WOMEN IN INDIAN MYTH, RITUAL AND HISTORY: THE *TAPASVINĪ* AND THE *VĪRĀṄGANĀ*

Kathryn Hansen

The Sanskrit noun for heroism, which continues to be used in many Indian languages today, is *vīrya*, or in its inflected form, *vīryam*. The hero is known as a *vīra*, *vīr*, or *bīr*, depending on the linguistic region. The concept of heroism cannot be glossed without reference to masculinity, insofar as vīryam is also commonly used with the meaning "semen." It appears that Brahminical culture in India constructed the masculine body as the site of virility and metaphorized its notion of heroism from the male organ's capacity for potency and firmness. From the outset, then, heroism or vīryam comes bundled as a gendered category.

Sanskrit treatises on aesthetics constructed another notion of heroism, as *vīra rasa*, one of the eight principal "moods" or "sentiments."[1] It is considered the backbone of the serious play or *nāṭaka*, the first of the ten hierarchically ordered genres of drama. In this genre, vīra rasa governs the actions and disposition of the male protagonist (*nāyaka*), prevailing over the amorous sentiments (*śṛṅgāra rasa*) that find their chief embodiment in the heroine. The bifurcation between the two chief rasas by gender extends far beyond the classical drama. Gender representation in Indian visual and performing arts to the present reproduces the dictum: women's bodies are the locus of eroticism, men's of heroism. Vīra rasa may be represented by a female dancer when she impersonates a male, as in solo recitals of Bharata Nāṭyam. However, the particular posture used to signal vīra rasa — or its concomitant traits of defiance, pride, and courage — signifies the code-switch when a female dancer takes on a male identity. It is rarely employed to invoke a female character, because heroic actions are not generally ascribed to women. Again, vīryam denotes masculinity; the male essence is synonymous with vīryam.

As this cursory exploration demonstrates, the problematic of a heroics of womanhood in India is inseparable from language and representation. Language constructs a gendered dichotomy that works to foreclose the possibility of representing women as heroes or heroic. Linguistic usage may also help us predict that if and when women are associated with the heroic, their femininity may be recoded and their gender identity elided with the masculine. This preliminary glance suggests how deeply embedded constructions of gender are in the symbolic systems that societies create and use. The intention is not to overlook the role of ideological factors or to assign priority to language over culture. Rather, it is to set the stage for a cultural study whose first axiom must be to assert the specificity of the group being studied. The overlapping boundaries of words and gender-loaded concepts reveal inscriptional practices that characterize a given people, offering insight into their distinct ways of negotiating more universal cultural problems.

The problem addressed in this essay is how women, a subordinated group whose agency is minimized through the institutional and ideological structures of patriarchy, in some contexts are seen and see themselves not simply as agents, but as *agents of heroic action.* The particular ways in which people of the Indian sub-continent have imagined and mythologized this problem are the focus of this essay. My method will be to reassemble the narratives, rituals, and histories of Indian women, many of which we may assume were scattered or suppressed as particular groups entrenched a dominant ideology of gender. In ferreting out the evidence of a womanly heroics in India, it is likely that we will not be recapitulating readily available themes. Given our preliminary findings, it seems we are going to have to unpack the dominant cultural images, seeking their inner structures, as well as look beyond them for conflicting evidence. Our task is a selective sifting, aiming for "retrieval of those cultural phenomena which express the repressed or alternate world views of women."[2]

This effort has the scholarly purpose of complementing the existing literature that focuses primarily on normative expectations of women in India. But it serves a practical, indeed political, purpose as well. For some time, women's activitists in both India and the West have been examining the cultural ideals conveyed through gender role models. The standards of womanly conduct set out in the stories, rituals, and songs preserved from the past have been found to shape the patterns of women's lives, their ideals and their orientation to social reality. While feminist Andrea Dworkin has analyzed the fairytale heroines Snow White, Sleeping Beauty, and Cinderella, all of whom "are characterized by passivity, beauty, innocence, and victimization,"[3] Indian activist Madhu Kishwar has expressed dismay at the notion of "woman as a selfless giver, someone who gives and gives endlessly, gracefully, smilingly, whatever the demand," as found in the mythological heroines Sītā, Sāvitrī, and Anusuyā.[4] In reconstituting India's heroic images of woman, one objective is to highlight material of use to women in the present historical moment. This paper hopes to contribute in some small way to the collective endeavour of reinterpreting indigenous traditions so as to reclaim exemplars of womanly action for ongoing struggles.

Several distinct patterns of heroic behavior among women weave through Indian myth, ritual, and history. Women acquire power and become capable of heroic action by adopting one or more of several heroic modes. Each is characterized by a specific vocabulary or discourse of heroism. The varieties of female heroism that I concentrate on in this essay are: 1) the *tapasvinī*, the self-denying woman who achieves power through the performance of *tapas*, ritualized acts of self-mortification; she exemp-

the *heroics of masochism*. 2) the *vīrāṅganā*, the warrior-woman
who takes revenge on foes in retribution for politically and
morally reprehensible deeds; she embodies the *heroics of conquest*. In a later publication, I intend to treat: 3) the *sādhvī*, the
female saint or guru who achieves autonomy by subordinating
herself only to God; she demonstrates the *heroics of transcen-
dence*. 4) the *devadāsī*, the courtesan skilled in the arts who
occupies a high position in the court or temple; she may be said
to engage a *heroics of performance*.

	In the discussion that follows, I isolate each of these heroic
modes and elaborate upon its manifestations through various
examples. The kinds of sources that supply illustrative evidence
include mythological stories, folk tales, songs, dramas, rituals,
and contemporary popular cultural media such as film. In more
than a few instances, I am indebted to scholars who have already
compiled information from such sources. While I deal with each
of the types initially in their "pure," highly contrastable forms, in
the second part of each section I examine historical leaders and
movements who incorporate these modes. Here I focus on the
reworking of preexisting definitions and creative appropriations
of the patterns laid down earlier.

	Throughout the discussion, I eschew the terminology of
"tradition" and "modernity," which describes women in undesir-
able ways. "Traditional" in reference to women is widely
employed to translate "normative." It is my aim to show that
non-normative as well as normative models of gendered conduct
have "traditions." The non-normative heroic paradigms for
women that I outline have histories of their own — however
fractured or buried. Further, as my narrative will indicate, these
paradigms are continuously being redefined as the representation
of woman is contested anew in each historical period.

Tapas and Strīdharma

The first category is, in a sense, the most obvious in that it proceeds from self-sacrifice, an important element in normative constructions of womanly behaviour. However, viewing self-sacrificial behavior as "heroic" is controversial, as many might choose to restrict their understanding of heroism to active resistance. Nonetheless, this mode of heroics is very much at the heart of female experience in India, and additionally has a religious and political ubiquity that cannot be ignored.

The heroics of masochism represents a passive form of heroism. This is the heroism of absorbing pain and injury rather than inflicting them. As the mode involving the least overt aggression, it is the most compatible with the ideology of woman as weak, long-suffering, and submissive and thus is easily overlooked as a site of heroism. The subversive potential of the concept, however, proceeds from its very appearance of propriety and innocence. A closer examination of the code of *strīdharma* (woman's duty) will show that although the heroics of masochism is based upon a conventional gender formulation, it may in certain cases, extend female agency into a larger domain.

Self-abnegation and subservience to the husband lie at the core of strīdharma, the normative code of behavior for high-caste Hindu women. As Katherine Young points out, "self-sacrifice has been a feminine mode of religiosity in most patriarchal religions, a mode which is related to the psychology of female subservience and male dominance."[5] In India, moreover, the centrality of sacrificial ritual to Vedic religion left its imprint on multiple social formations, including the evolving gender ideology. By the time of the epics and *dharmaśāstra*s (texts on proper behavior), the early valorization of the married woman as *sumaṅgalī* (fortunate) and *śiva* (auspicious) had been overlaid by emphasis on the wife's worship of the husband (*pati*) as god (*devatā*, but also pati, ambiguously meaning "lord").[6] As a sacrificer made offerings to the deities, so she was to offer up her devotion to her husband with the appropriate mental and physical attitudes of self-restraint, purification, and concentration. This ideal was termed *patiyoga* (*yoga* meaning "union," but also referring to the spiritual discipline of self-control) or *pativrātya* (the state of undertaking a *vrat*, a vow or fast, for one's husband, which is described below). Accordingly the husband was termed *patidevatā* (the husband/lord who is god).

Insofar as sacrifice was performed with the anticipation of benefit or merit for the sacrificer, the dutiful wife could expect to acquire rewards, even power, from the diligent discharge of strīdharma. Here the concept of *tapas*, central to Hindu asceticism, conflates with ideas of wifely subordination. Tapas literally means the "heat" generated by acts of self-suffering. This heat, created initially in the body, transmutes into energy or power that can be used to control persons, events, even gods. Numerous myths tell of saintly men, kings, and demons who performed austerities in order to gain power over their rivals. The *tapasvin*, the man who could sustain repeated acts of self-mortification, inspired awe and genuine fear because of his potential to wreak havoc in the lives of ordinary, dharma-abiding folk. What then of the *tapasvinī*, his female counterpart?

By the time of the dharmaśāstras, overt prohibitions on asceticism for women were common.[7] Eventually women were barred from the pursuit of *mokṣa* (spiritual liberation) and the fourth stage of life (*samnyāsa*) wherein mokṣa is the dominant goal, at least until the *bhakti* period. However, the relevance of the tapas model to the womanly ideal becomes obvious in the vast story literature found in the epics and Purāṇas. Here we see many examples of women's acts of sacrifice on behalf of their husbands bestowing upon them power, just as the ascetic's performance of tapas earned him his reward.

The epic heroine type — the wife who is sacrificing, chaste, loyal — still represents the ideal for female behavior, at least among the high Hindu castes.[8] Among the epic heroines, the most renowned are the trio Sāvitrī, Sītā, and Satī. The story of Sāvitrī shows that unswerving devotion to the husband, if faithfully practiced, can endow women with supernatural capacities, notably the power to bring back the dead. Passive endurance in adversity is the lesson imparted by Sītā, heroine of the *Rāmāyaṇa*, who follows Rāma into forest exile. Sītā gains the power to maintain her chastity even when captured by Rāvaṇa, and becomes the paragon of wifely virtue, although in the end she is repudiated by Rāma. Willingness to suffer even self-immolation for the preservation of the husband's honour is imparted by the example of Sītā's fire ordeal as well as the self-sacrifice of Satī, wife of Śiva. In each case, the heroine's self-sacrifice, like the ascetic's self-denial, leads to an accumulation of extraordinary merit or power.

Nonetheless, the prevailing gender hierarchy places definite limits on such feminine acts of tapas. The epic heroines sacrifice themselves for the sake of their husbands, not for their own benefit. Women who follow their example, it is held, should use the power acquired through their sufferings to secure the welfare, long life, and good name of the husband and the couple's offspring, particularly the sons. Elaborating on the virtue of subordinating self-sacrifice to conjugal obedience, an eighteenth century orthodox commentator, Tryambaka, states the relation between tapas and strīdharma concisely: "the ascetic practice [tapas] for women is the service of the husband by a devoted wife."[9] For Tryambaka, this equation implies the exclusion of women from performing austerities as a religious practice; tapas is listed as one of the six things that cause women to fall into hell, together with recitation of sacred texts, going on pilgrimages, renunciation, chanting of mantras, and worship of deities.[10] To the orthodox, tapas offers a helpful analogy for a woman's self-denying service to her husband, but insofar as it harbors a dangerous potential for heightening her status, it is rejected as a pursuit in itself.

Mythological and Ritual Sources for the Tapasvinī

Tryambaka's is a representative move to defuse tapas and discourage its appropriation by heroic women. Contesting this orthodox view, mythic and folk sources show married women succeeding in the practice of tapas, often against the objections of family and society. Most notable among them is Pārvatī, the consort of lord Śiva and tapasvinī par excellence. Pārvatī, sitting on a mountain-top exposed to the elements, performs prolonged acts of tapas to persuade Śiva to fall in love with her so that he will abandon his ascetic forswearal of sexuality. In Kālidāsa's poetic version of the story, the *Kumārasambhava*, Pārvatī's mother Menā tries to dissuade her, arguing, "What has tapas to do with your body?"[11] But Pārvatī takes off her jewels and rich robes and begins subsisting on forest produce. The particularly harsh acts of penance she performs include surrounding herself in summer with four blazing fires and gazing straight into the sun; breaking her fasting only with drops of dew; lying on stone amidst months of rain and wind; passing the nights of the cold season standing in water; refusing to eat even leaves that drop by themselves.[12] Pārvatī's ascetic valour finally impresses the ascetic god himself, who announces "I am your slave, gained by tapas."[13] The couple are married, and from their union is born Kārttikeya (Kumāra or Skanda), destined to conquer the demon Tāraka who has assumed supreme power over the worlds through his own accumulation of tapas.

This story illustrates the utmost resolve of which women are capable. Because Pārvatī's goal is physical union with Śiva, her actions may be read as paradigmatic for the courageous pursuit of feminine desire. However, it must be recalled that Pārvatī undertakes tapas only once, for the accomplishment of a specific end, and in most narrative and iconographic contexts is a gentle, gracious consort who domesticates Śiva and lives in peaceful wedded bliss with him. Pārvatī as tapasvinī is emulated by Śaivite devotees for her heroic endeavours to gain Śiva's

attention and blessing.[14]   But equally, she represents the
dharmapatnī, the wife whose perfect devotion to her lord the
worshipper strives to imitate. In other instances, she is the ideal
student, always ready to learn from her master Śiva.[15] Thus
while tapas generates martyr-like acts of self-control, enabling
women to demonstrate their heroism, the example of Pārvatī
would suggest that such heroics may be confined to the relatively
small, private space afforded women within marriage.

From this perspective, a Jain version of the *Rāmāyaṇa*, the
Padma Purāṇa discussed by Uma Chakravarti, offers an interesting twist on the self-sacrifice of the epic heroine Sītā.   In
Vālmīki's account of the *Rāmāyaṇa*, Sītā, after returning from
Lanka and living with Rāma in Ayodhya, was abandoned in the
forest because of public doubts about her chastity. Subsequently,
she endured a fire ordeal to prove her virtue. The Jain Sītā,
instead of agreeing to the ordeal, appeals to nature. Nature
responds by drenching Ayodhya in rains to quell the fire. As
floods rise on the city, the populace cries out to Sītā for help.
Sītā takes on a heroic posture; she rescues the city, renounces
Rāma, and becomes a *bhikṣuṇī*, a Jain nun. She enters the
renunciant path by plucking out each strand of her hair, "but
presumably even this extreme physical pain is preferable to a
humiliating existence with Rāma."[16] The heroics of masochism
serves here to underscore Sītā's fortitude and determination, also
acting as a public announcement of her self-willed separation
from her life of subservience to Rāma. Rather than using tapas to
gain a husband as Pārvatī does, the Jain Sītā mortifies herself to
gain liberation from him.

Penances may also be performed by wives for the sake of
offspring, as demonstrated in a Tamil folk epic, the *Aṇṇanmār
Katai* ("Brothers' Story" or "The Three Twins" as retold by
Brenda Beck). Tāmarai, the mother-to-be of the twin heroes, has
been informed by a soothsayer that she must perform a 21-year
penance to gain the favour of Śiva, who alone has the power to
impregnate her. Her tapas involves sitting on top of an elaborate

pillar made of seven balanced needles, topped by seven cups, topped by seven beads, seven more needles, and seven oleander flowers.[17] As she grows emaciated, bugs fill her hair and parrots nest in her nose; her braids become fixed to the four corners of the earth. When her accumulated tapas causes Śiva to suffer from a burning sensation, he orders her cut into small pieces, cast to the bottom of three hell pits, and trampled upon. Soon after, Viṣṇu revives her, but she must undergo a total of seven deaths before the ancestral curse of barrenness is removed.[18] Tāmarai's heroic acts qualify her to become the mother of heroes. Her voluntary sufferings give her the power not only to reverse her karma but to affect the karma of others through the agency of her curse.

In a typology of deities developed by Veena Das, goddesses who are associated with self-sacrifice and renunciation are generally encompassed within a higher male principle; they tend to be wives or consorts. Das notes the difference between the male and female performance of tapas: "The power of renunciation is well-recognised in Hindu myths. It often pits man against the gods and forces the latter to concede to the demands of men. However, the tapa (asceticism) of a woman is always *for* her husband, while the asceticism of a man takes him towards his own personal goals."[19] Whereas this formula applies to Pārvatī, Tāmarai, Vālmīki's Sītā, Sāvitrī, and others, it does not explain the Jain Sītā or other women who depart from Brahminical strīdharma. Rather than pursuing the latter, let us now look more closely at women's practices within upper-caste Hinduism, turning from mythological evidence to ethnography and ritual behavior. Can we rightly characterize female renunciatory heroics as exclusively husband- (or son-) oriented?

The gendered observance of *vrat*s provides the analogue in ritual life for the tapas of mythic lore. Vrats are ritual vows and the fasts, vigils, and religious readings connected with their undertaking. The vrat is carried out as a means of gaining power, of controlling and altering destiny. A vrat typically entails some penance or austerity, especially abstinence from food. During the undertaking of a vrat, the devotee makes a direct appeal to the deity by demonstrating faith and devotion through self-sacrifice. The objectives of the vrat are to reverse misfortune, remove sins (including those accrued in former lives), and gain favours or requests through the intercession of particular divinities. Vrats are commonly identified by the name of the deity being beseeched (Sāvitrī's vrat, Arundhatī's vrat, Santoshī Mā's vrat) or by the day on the ritual calendar when they are performed (Ṛṣi Pañcamī, Putradā Ekādaśī).

By the early medieval period, the vrat had become extremely popular as a religious practice open to all castes and both sexes.[20] In modern India however, vrats are primarily observed by women,[21] and as such they have been the subject of recent scholarship on distinctive female cultural and religious domains. Whereas medieval male commentators classified the vrat as an "optional" activity and included spiritual liberation as one of the reasons for performing it, twentieth-century women view it as *nitya* or as a necessary part of strīdharma.[22] In a survey of 108 women in Maharashtra, Mary McGee found that "marital felicity" (*saubhāgya*), the health and long life of the husband, the health and long life of the children, and the acquisition of progeny were the reasons the largest number of women gave for performing vrats, while the women's own health and prosperity were listed less than half the time and mokṣa appeared near the bottom.[23] Another important distinction is that when a vrat is undertaken by a woman, the merit or benefits gained are commonly transferred to a family member, e.g. the husband or perhaps a son or daughter. Men may also perform vrats for the welfare of their families, but in practice this occurs less often, and there are no ready examples of the transfer of vrat-earned merit from husband to wife.

The performance of vrats is inculcated in unmarried girls and becomes an important tool for socialization into the attitudes and customs of strīdharma. Shudha Mazumdar, an upper class

Bengali woman born in 1899, tells in her memoirs how she was introduced as a child to simple *brata*s for the tulsī plant and the cow, followed by her first formal participation in a brata for lord Śiva when she was eight. Her mother regularly performed the arduous Sāvitrī brata, which required three days of fasting and prayer in the scorching month of June; women who successfully completed the rite fourteen years in a row were blessed with the boon acquired by Sāvitrī, to "never know the dread pangs of widowhood."[24] The chastening effect of vrat-performance is illustrated by the special selection of the Madhu-Saṅkrānti brata for Shudha. Her childish propensity for angry retorts was to be corrected by her monthly presentation of a bowl of honey to a holy man for two years: "it was hoped that by his blessings I would gain a honeyed tongue."[25]

Among high-caste women of Nepal, as described by Lynn Bennett, voluntary religious fasts or *barta*s are undertaken on a weekly or monthly basis and are very popular. "On any given Sunday, Tuesday, new moon, or full moon day (as well as countless other auspicious days during the year) one would find many Narikot women abstaining from their regular meals and taking only a little fruit or milk in order to earn merit."[26] Other ascetic activities favoured by women include sexual abstinence, all-night vigils, and vows of silence; all are considered extremely powerful. According to Bennett, these exercises in self-control and abstinence are ideologically equated with the tapas performed by ascetics, for both the household and the ascetic use austerity to gain "purity/power."[27] Her bracketing of the concepts purity and power is particularly suggestive of the way in which strīdharma intersects with feminine desire. She observes that women pursue their own private strategies as well as publicly accepted roles when they perform wifely acts of service or self-denial.

Bennett's ethnographic work suggests that austerities and devotional acts like vrats may be used by women to enhance their familial and societal position. By showing devotion to their husbands, women win the male favour necessary for securing their position in the household.[28] Demonstrations of obedience and piety may therefore arise not solely from concern for the husband's welfare (the articulated goal), but from the desires of the wife (unspoken and unarticulated), such as the wish for survival, safety, and even advancement. Through the performance of public rituals, women further gain influence in the community, enhancing their prestige.[29] Women's use of rituals of self-abnegation to secure their own ends is most vividly illustrated in the practices connected with worshipping the husband's feet. A respectful wife demonstrates patrifocal deference by washing her husband's feet and drinking the "foot water" before each meal. In private, however, a woman may undertake the "devotional" act of rubbing oil on her husband's feet as a prelude to sex, moving her hands from the feet up the calves to the thighs.[30] Bennett reports, "Women told me frankly that sex, as the means to have children and as the means to influence their husband in their favor, was their most effective weapon in the battle for security and respect in their husband's house."[31]

McGee similarly argues that although few women admit to observing vrats for their own benefit, the practice of female rituals ensures women's welfare as well as men's.[32] A wife's respect, self-esteem, and good fortune depend upon the survival and prosperity of her husband and sons. Her fasts and rites are not surprisingly oriented at preserving the very things that enhance her own status, or in warding off the misfortunes that threaten to destroy it. Returning then to Veena Das' perception that women's tapas is directed toward the benefit of others, especially male kin, it appears that the causes and effects of this form of heroics are more complex. Patriarchal ideology explicitly directs women to sacrifice themselves for others, but this does not rule out the possibility that women's desires overlap with concern for male kin. Nor does it preclude the use of self-deprivational tactics for purely personal goals. Any mode of heroism has the potential to endow its agent with authority; the heroics of female masochism is no different. Regardless of the orientation toward self and/or other (which for women is probably a falsely posed dichotomy), by undertaking self-willed acts of denial, women step into a heroic role. When the tapasvinī subordinates herself to her "lord," she simultaneously masters her ego. Paradoxically, as she demonstrates her acceptance of this heroic side of strīdharma, she becomes a participant in constructing her own identity and destiny.

The puzzled feminist reader may lose patience unless I restate my position at this point. In suggesting the possibility of locating female agency within myths and rituals that entail self-denial, I do not mean to erase the privations and denigration suffered by women due to patriarchal religious ideologies that valorize self-sacrifice. I am not embarking on an apology for strīdharma nor advocating that women today revive penitential practices. What I am hoping to stimulate is a wider discussion of the ways in which women use the cultural resources available to them to gain strength. The male-dominated institutional structures in any society set up barriers that effectively prevent women from converting their accumulation of self-control into genuine power. The tapasvinī model, insofar as it operates primarily within the context of marriage, is particularly limited in this regard. Nonetheless, the ascetic practices that underlie a major part of Hindu philosophical thought have tended to privilege the performer of tapas. Women's sufferings, I simply point out, are often tinged with the aura of the heroic. The noble appearance of pain may be rejected by the feminist as phony or manipulated, but it may also be capitalized upon by the sufferer and manipulated for her own ends. Perhaps more importantly, it is also frequently appropriated by men who claim ownership of women as wives or kin and stand to benefit in social or economic ways from their moral purity.

Satī and Satyāgraha

With this aside, let us tenuously proceed to consider the most extreme form of female self-suffering, the act of self-immolation termed suttee or *sati*. This contentious topic has been treated at length by a number of authors, and my purpose is a restricted one by comparison.[33]   It is just to assert that the concept of sati belongs on the same ideological continuum with tapas and vrats as a heroic form of female self-suffering. It would be irresponsible to argue that sati as a historical practice enlarged women's agency, and I do not wish to imply anything of that sort. I include sati in this discussion because the woman who commits ritual self-willed death has been glorified and venerated in past representations; indeed, she continues to be viewed as an ideal woman and/or goddess by certain groups in India. Explaining the persistence of sati, I believe, is difficult without understanding the ideological dimension that lends heroic stature to the satī's image.

It may be helpful to note that the goddess Satī (with whom the practice is linked) was Śiva's first wife, and Pārvatī (Śiva's second wife) was her reincarnation. Satī/Pārvatī are equated in the popular perception, both sharing similar narrative and visual representations as tapasvinī. As with Pārvatī, Satī's devotion and asceticism attract Śiva's attention, and he grants her a boon for her austerities leading to their marriage.[34] The incident that provokes Satī's suicide, however, bears little resemblance to the conditions under which a Hindu wife commits sati. According to the myth, some time after their marriage, Satī is outraged at her father Dakṣa's refusal to invite Śiva and herself to a great sacrifice. In protest at the insult, she kills herself *while Śiva is still alive*. Satī's self-sacrifice causes Śiva to grieve so intensely that the cosmos is threatened with disruption. In contrast, the woman who undertakes sati follows her husband to death, theoretically because *her* grief at separation from her husband is too great to bear. The idea of a wife killing herself *before* her husband and thereby causing him to suffer seems quite contrary to strīdharma. As David Kinsley points out, "Satī's suicide, although perhaps the act of a faithful wife who cannot endure insults to her husband, results not in her maintaining a relationship with her husband but in her breaking that relationship."[35] Although the goddess Satī is associated with the practice of sati, Kinsley concludes that Satī's suicide may not provide its mythological paradigm.

The word satī comes from *sat* or *satya*, "truth, virtue." Satī (in its adjectival form, "she who is truthful") is a term applied to the wife who follows strīdharma, that is, the virtuous female who is loyal and self-sacrificing. Sat or "truth" in the context of women's narratives generally signifies chastity and physical inviolability. By dying prior to, together with, or immediately after her husband, a satī preserves the sexual fidelity to her spouse that is his entitlement and that constitutes his and his family's honour. The preservation of female purity through self-sacrifice is thus central to the ideology of sati. Even the widow who does not commit sati is bound by it. The state of widowhood assumes the same code of sexual fidelity, remarriage being forbidden for women. The widow is deprived of all the marks of auspicious womanhood that might make her desirable to men, is ostracized socially, and is required to subject herself to an ascetic withdrawn mode of existence. Because of the harshness of widowhood, many have claimed that the surviving female chooses sati as a preferable path.

The notion of sat, grounded in the ideology of wifely loyalty and chastity, takes the form of a supernatural power in folk beliefs. In rural Rajasthan, sat is understood as a force that possesses women and gives them extraordinary powers.[36] Women possessed by sat have special capabilities: to curse, to grant boons, to prophesy, to cure diseases, and most importantly, to will the funeral pyre to light by itself and to endure its flames without pain. While all women strive for a generalized condition of sat or feminine virtue, sat in this specific usage describes a rarely attained perfection that activates the transformation of an ordinary woman into a goddess. As Kumkum Sangari and Sudesh Vaid explain, "The woman possessed with *sat* is separated from past self, shorn of her individuality.... These no longer matter, she is practically a *devī* .... The belief in *sat* thus elevates what would otherwise be seen as suicide or ritualised murder into a supremely holy act."[37] Of course, the correct determination of a woman's sat is possible only after the fact, once the act of sati has been concluded. As Sangari and Vaid indicate, the villagers' assertions of the presence of sat construct a particular explanation of events that minimizes their own collaboration and culpability in what Sangari and Vaid view as a less than voluntary act.

Other modes of interpretation for the occurrence of sati, especially material ones, compete with these views even within the local context. Contemporary secular commentators ascribe the performance of sati to a combination of psychological pressure on the widow, manipulation by family members, and physical coercion, rather than supernatural causes. The larger factors discussed to explain sati include almost every form of societal tension, from military insecurity and threat of conquest (which led women to collective acts of suicide known as *jauhar* while their men were in battle), to competition in agricultural society for prestige, prevention of widows' inheritance of property, exploitation by priests, and recently threats to gender relations posed by education and meddling of political parties.[38]

Perhaps part of the problem for scholars lies in squaring the horror of sati as reconstructed in our imaginations with the adulation accruing to the satī as idealized woman/goddess in indigenous culture. Here perhaps a return to the vocabulary of female heroism may offer some insight. The admiration, indeed glorification, that distinguishes the woman who commits sati can be grasped by situating sati within a spectrum of sacrificial deeds, wherein it is both the most public and final way in which a faithful wife can demonstrate her heroic endurance. The satī is deified because her acts — like those of Pārvatī, Sītā, Sāvitrī and other goddesses — represent the normative achievement of self-sacrifice carried to an heroic extreme. From this perspective, her pain is quite real and is, in fact, necessary as proof of her suffering, even though the complicity of others in creating it may be erased by reference to the supernatural power of sat. It is precisely because she suffers, because she is courageous in the face of death, that she is celebrated as a model tapasvinī and is widely lauded in folk legend and belief.

Uma Chakravarti has explored how a golden age of Indian womanhood was constructed in response to the British colonial ideology of moral and cultural superiority, with its foregrounding of "the Aryan woman (the progenitor of the upper- caste woman) as the *only* object of historical concern."[39] She notes that in fictional representations by Indian authors of the late 19th century, strong women characters of the past were valorized for their dual roles as dutiful partners and heroic self-sacrificers. Both aspects, I suggest, belong to the tapasvinī mode associated with Pārvatī/Satī. R.C. Dutt's novels, for example, told of brave warriors who would restore martial values to Indian culture, a preparatory stage for the unwritten but anticipated eventual confrontation with and defeat of the British. In *Pratap Singh*, Dutt lauded the female counterparts of the Rajput heroes as "models of wisdom, indomitable courage and undying resistance." Central to the women's heroic identity was the test of valour contained in the performance of sati, usually undertaken even as their husbands rode off to battle, freeing them from the worry of dishonour to family and clan.[40]

Interestingly, Chakravarti shows how the "glory" of the woman who becomes a satī was also propagated by colonial writers who professed to scholarly motives. H.T. Colebrooke, considered the "greatest Oriental scholar that England has ever produced" by Max Müller,[41] wrote his first essay "On the Duties of the Faithful Hindu Widow" in 1794. Among its many consequences was the circulation of the image of the burning woman as icon of an admired, indeed "awesome" concept of Indian womanhood.[42] The image was reinforced by travellers' accounts and contributed to the mystique of the exotic Oriental female. European women such as Mrs. Speier who wrote *Life in Ancient India* (1856) were deeply impressed by the historical accounts of satīs, and even though the practice had been banned, they still viewed it as "inspiring," and "the ultimate power that the Hindu woman had in an otherwise powerless situation."[43] In this way, indigenous and colonial interests contributed to the remaking of the past and present of "the Indian woman," such that her capacity for loyalty and self-sacrifice were equated with her high-caste Aryan origins. In the process, sati was revalorized as an heroic act in the popular imagination of both the colonizers and the colonized.

The practice of self-immolation has been appropriated in recent times as a strategy of political protest without restriction by gender. The suicides by Buddhist monks during the Vietnam War became world-famous through globally transmitted photographs and televised news reports. In India in 1990, during massive student protests against the implementation of the Mandal Commission Report, which proposed extension of quotas for government jobs to members of the "Other Backward Castes" (OBCs), scores of young people doused themselves with kerosene and set themselves aflame. Those who succeeded in killing themselves became instant heroes, and were said in the press to have inspired other students to emulate their bravery.

Perhaps the most influential application of the heroics of masochism, with its unique merger of self-sacrifice (tapas) and truth (sat, satya), is found in the political philosophy of Mahatma Gandhi, the leader who brought independence to India. Gandhi's principle of *satyāgraha* entailed apprehension of truth or moral rectitude and adherence to it in belief and behaviour. The best method for engaging in satyāgraha was through the concentrated focus of mind and body brought about by saintly tapas. In his own life, Gandhi gradually incorporated more and more attributes of the ascetic lifestyle, even as he conferred with world leaders and led his followers on countless campaigns. He adopted a code of celibacy and vegetarianism, wore minimal clothing, and enjoyed few physical comforts. He spent long periods in solitary fasting and meditation, searching for the insight to resolve national problems and tame his own desires. In his political practice, he perfected techniques of non-violent resistance that have been adopted by political leaders around the world. Rather than attempting to confront the British rulers and defeat them through force, Gandhi exhorted the Indian populace to assert its moral superiority by simultaneously protesting against injustice and voluntarily submitting to arrest, beatings, and imprisonment. He thus attempted to convert the strategic weakness of the Indian masses into their greatest strength, achieving power through passive suffering.

As Katherine Young has pointed out, Gandhi's satyāgraha was cognate with strīdharma in its broad outlines.[44] His vows and fasts were comparable to women's vratas; his jail sentences were self-imposed tapas; his salt marches and extensive travel by foot resembled the tīrthayātrās (pilgrimages) undertaken often by older Hindu women. Like a woman upholding her sat, he insisted on physical purity. But he went even further than a virtuous women, for he avoided sexual relations with his wife after a point. Gandhi appropriated the heroic vocabulary of feminine religious culture because he recognized within it strategies for attaining power that could be directly transferred to the encounter with the British.

British domination of India had long been inscribed in Western representation by means of the gendered metaphor of the masculine active Europe ruling over the feminine passive East. According to Ashish Nandy, the homology between sexual and political dominance was invariably used by Western colonial powers, whether in Asia, Africa, or Latin America.[45] Gandhi played up to the hyper-masculinity of the West, confronting it with the self-mastery and power latent in Indian femininity. That the passive heroic mode was at first misread as a manifestation of the "inscrutable East" was perhaps a foregone conclusion, but this did not diminish the effectiveness of Gandhi's strategy. Nandy suggests that Gandhi reordered colonial culture's hierarchy of sexual identities, reversing the domination of *puruṣatva* (manliness) over *nārītva* (womanliness). He introduced a new formulation of femininity as superior to masculinity, or, in another reading, an alternate ordering in which manliness and womanliness are equal but the ability to transcend the man-woman dichotomy is superior.[46]

Since Gandhi's politics deployed the tactics that Indian women had long used in the domestic sphere, his brand of nationalism made an especially loud call to women, who joined his campaigns in large numbers in both South Africa and India. Women easily made the transition from the self-denial practiced in everyday contexts to the purposeful suffering enjoined by satyāgraha.[47] Gandhi redirected their self-sacrifice from husband to nation, transforming the satī into the *satyāgrahinī*. He urged their participation in the nationalist struggle, praising women's "nobility" and heightened capacity for self-sacrifice. He even expressed a hope that more women than men would follow him, for this would ensure that violence would be avoided.[48] While Gandhi's attitudes on women were complex and often contradictory, there is little doubt that he enabled large numbers of Indian women to leave their homes to participate in the independence movement, and through this participation they became more emancipated. Gandhian politics and philosophy had a significant influence on those pre-Independence women who are now understood to have constituted the first phase of Indian feminism, while the orientation of those early fighters continues to shape the course of the women's movement in its current second phase.

The Vīrāṅganā and Her Mythic Forbears

Alongside the tapasvinī exists an overlooked and yet important alternative paradigm of Indian womanhood: the *vīrāṅganā*, the woman who manifests the qualities of vīryam or heroism. The vīrāṅganā seems to be a paradox within the normative categories for gender in high-caste Hindu society. She is a valiant fighter who distinguishes herself by prowess in warfare, an activity normally reserved for men. She demonstrates her martial skills and courage by direct participation in combat, at the risk of her life; in fact, sometimes she dies in battle or takes her own life on the battlefield to avoid ignominious defeat. She is a leader of women and men, acting as head of state during peace and general in time of war. She adopts male attire, as well as the symbols of male status and authority, especially the sword, and she rides a horse. The vīrāṅganā is dedicated to virtue, wisdom, and the defence of her people. Above all, she is a fighter and a victor in the struggle with the forces of evil.

Folklore and mythology provide many examples of women of this type, especially the non-elite forms: local legends, folk theatre, popular song. The evidence for the vīrāṅganā includes the historical record, which documents the existence of outstanding queens in various regions of India since ancient times. The twentieth century descendants of the vīrāṅganā are represented in the valiant women of the popular cinema and in the "bandit queen." These heroines are also the topics of comic books, children's literature, and school texts. The vīrāṅganā ideal has been adopted by political and social reform movements, and the prototype has undergone change with historical and cultural developments. The abundance of examples suggests that the vīrāṅganā, while not the dominant norm for the high castes of North India, has had a continuous presence for many centuries as a mode of female heroism. It is a unique vision of womanhood, combining direct assumption of power with exemplary virtue.

Examples of the vīrāṅganā exist in many parts of India, and one suspects that the type, if not the nomenclature, is not restricted to the South Asian sub-continent. The warrior-woman was undoubtedly a more common phenomenon in the tribal cultures situated on the periphery of the central Indian cultural zone, particularly in the matrilineal cultures that existed before the advent of the Indo-Aryans and still flourish in the mountainous areas. However, this section will primarily examine the vīrāṅganā in North India, primarily in the Indo-Gangetic plain, although this means neglecting famous figures such as Rānī Chennammā of Karnataka. Hence the picture to be sketched may be magnified to fit the broader canvas of South Asia, yet in itself it tells much about the counter-culture of womanhood that existed and still exists in the heartland of Sītā and Sāvitrī.

We have seen that the tapasvinī model is linked with the goddess in her benign aspect as Pārvatī/Satī, who subordinates herself to her husband and performs the functions of the dutiful wife. In Hindu mythology, goddesses also exist who stand alone or, if related to men, are viewed as mothers. Here the goddess exercises distinctive female control through the ability to generate and nurture life. She is said to possess *śakti*, "energy" or "power" which has both procreative and destructive potentials. If such a goddess is allied to a male deity, her śakti becomes his activating principle. Thus Lakṣmī in the Pāñcarātra school is considered the śakti or stimulating force behind Viṣṇu, the creator, who is inactive without her intervention.[49] In some philosophical traditions, the individual goddesses may be considered manifestations of an overarching energy principle or great deity Śakti.

The mythology of Durgā, best-known of the śakti goddesses, is the most relevant for an investigation of the female heroics of conquest. Durgā is a warrior queen whose primary function is to combat demons who threaten the cosmos. She is depicted with many arms, each of which wields a weapon. Riding a fierce lion, she is said to be indestructible in battle.[50] Her

most popularly known contest occurs with the buffalo demon
Mahiṣa, who after performing tapas earned the boon of becoming
invincible except at the hands of a woman. The gods combine
their collective inner strengths in the form of heat and fire and
create Durgā to resolve the cosmic crisis. Durgā's most frequently depicted icon shows her slaying Mahiṣa with her raised sword.
In the various tales that relate the battle, she decapitates Mahiṣa
singlehandedly or with the help of female warriors whom she calls
forth from her own śakti: bloodthirsty, menacing goddesses such
as Kālī and the seven Mātṛkās (mothers).

As Kinsley notes, Durgā violates the normative models for
women. "She is not submissive, she is not subordinated to a male
deity, she does not fulfill household duties, and she excels at what
is traditionally a male function, fighting in battle. As an independent warrior who can hold her own against any male on the
battlefield, she reverses the normal role for females.... Durgā
does not lend her power or śakti to a male consort but rather *takes*
power from the male gods in order to perform her own heroic
exploits."[51] When approached by male suitors, Durgā rejects
their offers with threats and combative language. She is beautiful
and attractive to men but resists all attempts by men to take her
under their protection. Her beauty, in fact, lures them into the
trap of their own destruction.

A related warrior goddess, Kālī, partakes of a number of
Durgā's attributes but is more fearful and destructive by nature.
Represented as an emaciated, gruesome figure with fangs for teeth
and a protruding tongue, she wears a garland of severed heads
around her neck. Kālī symbolizes death in its terrifying aspect
more than does Durgā; she, too, is an invincible warrior. She
frequents the battlefield where she is a furious fighter and is fond
of drinking her victims' blood, as well as the cremation ground
where she frolics with corpses and ghouls. Sometimes she is
associated with Śiva, although when she, rather than Pārvatī, is
his consort, Śiva becomes wild and uncontrollable. In other
settings, she is depicted standing or dancing on Śiva's dead or

inert body in a pose of domination. Kālī and Durgā are also called Caṇḍī or Caṇḍikā, Cāmuṇḍā, and a host of other epithets.[52] All of these forms of the goddess share the iconography of weaponry, war, conquest, and the aftermath of battle — death.

Worship of Durgā or her equivalent forms has become a general feature of popular Hinduism in certain parts of India, most notably Bengal, but particular groups also favour Durgā, especially kings, warriors, and bandits. Durgā was worshipped by the Pāṇḍavas in the *Mahābhārata* and by lord Rāma before their epic battles. Since the 10th century, Kālī has been the patron goddess of thieves and thugs.[53] An 11-12th c. Jain text by Somadeva connects the worship of the goddess Aparājitā or Ambikā, who gives victory in war and is present in the king's weapons, with Mahānavamī, the last day of Durgā Pūjā.[54] Rulers such as Śivājī, the 17th c. Marathi leader, received their swords from the goddess and showed their respects by naming the weapons after her. In the 19th century, Abbé Dubois described the worship of weapons in Mysore during Dasarā (the festival immediately following Durgā Pūjā), while Alexander Forbes wrote of similar practices among the Rajputs.[55] In present-day India, the Navarātri or Durgā Pūjā festival celebrates Durgā's eminence, its tenth day of Dassarā (Dasherā, Dasserā) commemorating the goddess' victory over demon Mahiṣa. The festival has become an important occasion for rulers to worship the goddess for success in battle. In Nepal, the festival dedicated to Durgā is called Dasai. The *khukuri* (long curved dagger) is worshipped together with "nine Durgās," nine types of cutting implements owned by the family, with daily offerings and readings to the goddess in the festival of Navarātri.[56] An important part of these autumnal festivals is the ritual decapitation of an animal such as a goat or a buffalo whose blood is offered as a sacrifice to the goddess.

In the mythology and folklore of South India, many examples arise of women taking on an aggressive heroic stance when angered or wronged. Although the heroine Kannakī plays the part of a long-suffering, dutiful wife throughout most of the Tamil epic *Cilappatikāram*, in the end she expresses her outrage at her husband's wrongful execution by ripping off her breast and burning up the city of Madurai, following which she is transformed into a goddess. In an opposite developmental pattern, the goddess Mīnākṣī is brought up as a boy and ascends her father's throne upon his death. She undertakes a campaign to conquer the world, proceeding all the way to Mount Kailasa, lord Śiva's abode. Seeing the ascetic god, she is smitten with love and modesty, and abandons her powerful battle guise to become a demure wife.[57] In another story, a sort of Tamilian folk sequel to the *Rāmāyaṇa*, Sītā herself goes into battle against a hundred-headed form of the demon Rāvaṇa. She calls upon monkey-leader Hanumān to organize her army, and together with the forces of 56 countries, they cross six seas; eventually a great battle ensues.[58] The examples of South Indian goddesses doing battle against hostile demons could be multiplied many times over.

Vīrānganās from Indian History

Turning now to the historical record, the vīrānganā appears from time to time in exceptional female leaders who prevailed amidst the circumstances of their times to rise to visible positions of power. India's warrior queens have retained a strong grip on the imagination and have been the subjects of stories, legends, poems and songs down through the ages. What follows is a popular history of the vīrānganās of North India, based not upon primary historical documents but on the much-circulated accounts that represent contemporary views. Although the discussion up to now has limited itself to Hindu conceptions of heroic womanhood, I will cite some examples of non-Hindu women as well, because they have been assimilated within popular memory into the vīrāṅganā type and share the warrior-woman profile.

Razia Sultānā was the first and only woman of the Sultanate (or any later period) to ascend the throne at Delhi. She was the daughter of Iltutmish, the powerful ruler of the Slave dynasty. Her father had a special fondness for her as a child and trained her himself in politics and affairs of state. She was well-versed in the *Qurān*, knew several other sciences, and demonstrated her martial courage in various campaigns early in life. She was chosen over her brothers to take charge of the administration for several years while Iltutmish conducted military excursions to the south. Her father then designated her heir-apparent on the basis of her competence and experience, and following his death, she established herself on the throne even though her mother supported the claims of her brother Ruknuddīn Firoz.

Razia's accession raised questions about the right of females to enjoy sovereign power, a practice known to the Turks and Persians but new to India. For some time Razia was able to neutralize the factions which challenged her authority. She appeared daily on the imperial throne in male attire. According to Sir H. Elliot, "She discarded her female apparel and veil, wore a tunic and cap like a man, gave public audience, and rode on an elephant without any attempt at concealment."[59] She was involved in several battles against rebellious Turkish nobles and was finally captured and put to death while a prisoner. In all, she was the sovereign ruler for four years (1236-1240).

Many of the characteristics of Razia's career are found in the later vīrāṅganās known to history: her early tutelage by her father; her education in both the arts of war and the skills of reading, writing, and administration; her rise to power at the death of a male kinsman; her reputation as a wise, just and generous ruler; her assumption of male costume and perquisites of royal office; her military leadership and valour in defending her kingdom against enemies; her death in battle. But while Razia was named heir-apparent by her father, it was more common for royal women to ascend the throne while serving as regents for their underage sons. Queen-regents ruled among the Rajputs, Muslims, Marathas, and Gonds, as we shall soon see.

What is significant about the queen-regent is the rejection of the practice of sati implied in this role. These queens chose not to immolate themselves upon their husbands' deaths, defying the code of female virtue through self-sacrifice. Instead they assumed power and ruled in place of male offspring until the age of majority (and sometimes beyond). Several stories of such queens emphasize the decision to forego sati, with its promise of earthly prestige and spiritual liberation, for the greater obligation of serving one's family and one's people in the face of hostile threats.

Once in office, such queens did not stint in the defence of their kingdoms. When Samar Singh of Chitor was vanquished in the second battle of Tarain against Mu'īzuddīn Muhammad in 1192, his queen Kurmā Devī stood in for the minor heir, Karan. Possessed of military valour and skill in administration, she "nobly maintained what his father left. She headed her Rajputs and gave battle in person to Kutubuddīn, near Amber, when the viceroy was defeated and wounded."[60]

A similar story is that of Rānī Durgāvatī, a favorite judging from the amount of detail included in the various sources. Rānī Durgāvatī ruled among the Gonds of what is now Madhya Pradesh at the time of the emperor Akbar. The sources differ as to her origins, but several say that she was the daughter of the Chandella Rajput chief of Mahoba. Father and daughter were fond of riding and hunting together. Her marriage to Dalpat Shāh, the king of Gondwana, represented an interracial alliance, and this element has been used to construct a modern-day image of her as a high-minded, forward-thinking reformer, struggling with the society's prejudices and the opposition of a caste-conscious father. Soon after she gave birth to a son, Bīr Nārāyaṇ, her husband died and she became regent.[61] Early on, she had to face several attacks on her kingdom, and she success-fully repulsed the incursions of Bāz Bahādur of Malwa. The legends about her skill in tiger-hunting appear to have their origin in Abul Fazl's account: "She was a good shot with gun and arrow, and continually went a-hunting and shot animals of the chase with her gun. It was her custom that whenever she heard that a tiger had made his appearance she did not drink water till she had shot him."[62] She was also known for her wise counsel and munificence, and while she ruled there were no rebellions in her kingdom.

Durgāvatī's challenge came with the advance of Akbar's imperial army under the leadership of Asaf Khān. Cloaked in armour, mounted on an elephant, "with her bow and quiver lying by her side and with a burnished lance in her hand, the Rani herself led the troops," even in opposition to the advice of her officers.[63] She inflicted two defeats on the Mughal invaders, but in a third contest her badly outnumbered forces became demoralized when her son was wounded, and they deserted the field. At this point, Durgāvatī continued the fight on her elephant, sustaining a series of wounds, and she finally stabbed herself when capture seemed imminent. Thus ended her fifteen or sixteen years of regency, and according to the *Central Provinces Gazetteer*, her death in 1564 was "as noble and devoted as her life had been useful."[64]

While Abul Fazl celebrated the virtues of Durgāvatī in the *Akbarnāmah*, another queen-regent of the same period, Chānd Bībī of Ahmadnagar, also resisted the Mughal advance and was lauded by generations of historians as well as luminaries like Annie Besant. As she reigned in the Deccan, outside the geo-graphical focus of this section, we will only recapitulate a few points that link her with the other vīrānganās. Daughter of Husain Nizām Shāh and sister of Burhān-ul-mulk, she was well-trained in Arabic and Persian and spoke several Deccani languages. She participated equally with her husband Alī Ādil Shāh in both military and administrative affairs while he was alive, and when he died, she succeeded to the throne of Bijapur and became regent for his nephew. One famous anecdote relates to the siege of the Ahmadnagar fort by the Mughals shortly before her death in 1599:

> Once, when a portion of the rampart was blown away by mines laid by the besiegers, she rushed out of her palace barefooted with a number of trusted followers, a veil on her face and a naked sword in her hand, and rallying her men succeeded in repairing the damaged wall overnight.[65]

In honour of her bravery, the Mughal prince Murād bestowed on her the title Chānd Sultānā, and withdrew his troops. Like Razia Sultānā, she fell victim in the end to dissensions among her own nobles.

The story of Tārābāī, wife of Prithvīrāj, as recounted in Colonel Tod's *Annals and Antiquities of Rajasthan*, offers an example of the valour achieved by certain Rajput queens in the sixteenth century. Tārābāī was the daughter of a deposed chief, Rāī Surtān, whose lifelong ambition was to regain his kingdom at Thoda. Trained by her father in sports and the use of the bow and spear, at fourteen, "scorning the habiliments and occupations of her sex, she dressed pretty much like her father's cavaliers, learned to guide the war-horse, and to throw with unerring aim the arrow from his back even while at full speed."[66] Tārābāī and her father made an attempt to recapture Thoda from the Afghans but failed, and subsequently it was declared that whoever accomplished the deed would win her hand in marriage. Prithvīrāj's brother Jaimal proceeded to court her, but when he tried to dishonour her in the palace, he was killed by her father. Prithvīrāj then stepped in and declared his intention to become her husband. Riding with Tārābāī at his side, the two (with only one cavalryman) infiltrated a Muslim procession in Thoda and struck down the Afghan chief: Prithvīrāj dealt a blow with his lance while Tārābāī delivered the fatal wound with an arrow from her bow. She then killed an elephant singlehandedly, enabling the couple to escape safely. "The exploit ... won the hand of the fair Amazon, who, equipped with bow and quiver, subsequently accompanied him in many perilous enterprises."[67] Tārābāī did not rule in her own right, although she defended her kingdom on a number of occasions. When Prithvīrāj was later poisoned, she joined him on the funeral pyre as a satī.

The rule of Ahalyābāī Holkar in Maharashtra in the eighteenth century lasted thirty years, and in this queen we find the virtues of just and efficient administration carried to the highest point. Married at the age of eight to Khanḍujī (or Khanḍe Rāo), son of Malhār Rāo Holkar, Ahalyābāī was trained for her future duties by her father-in-law rather than her father; "he coached her in the collection of revenue, writing of dispatches and in the management of the army. Many a time he also took her with him in his campaigns."[68] In addition to learning to ride, wield weapons, and exercise the arts of statecraft, she was educated in the Hindu scriptures and later showed great interest in religious texts. Before she was twenty, her husband was killed during an expedition on which Ahalyābāī, Malhār Rāo, and Khanḍe Rāo had embarked. Ahalyā decided to become a satī, but Malhār Rāo dissuaded her.[69] She began to assume more and more of the responsibilities of rulership. Malhār Rāo's death soon followed, and Ahalyābāī's son Male Rāo was named head of the government, but he was mentally unstable and died shortly thereafter.

Ahalyābāī thus took complete control of the reins of administration in 1765 and ruled until her death in 1795, assisted by Tukojī Rāo, an adopted son who was in charge of the army. During the early stage of her reign, she prevented an attack by Raghobā by organizing a regiment of women, preparing her troops for combat, and displaying herself in command, "directing four bows, with quivers full of arrows, to be fitted to the corners of the howdah, or seat, on her favourite elephant."[70] She also quelled uprisings by the Chandravat Rajputs and the Bhils, personally leading her forces. After these initial challenges, her country enjoyed peace for a long period. "The undisturbed internal tranquility of the country was even more remarkable than its exemption from foreign attack," wrote Sir John Malcolm in 1832.[71]

She sat every day in open court, transacting business and distributing justice, investigating even the smallest appeals in detail. Unlike the other vīrāṅganās, she was not commonly pictured in male dress, but instead wore simple widow's attire, plain white clothing without any jewelry except a small necklace. Ahalyabai's rule was marked by an increase in the prosperity of her people, moderate taxation, stability in the ministerial ranks, the construction of highways, forts, wells, and temples, acts of charity directed to the poor and Brahmins, and a high level of piety in her personal life. Lauded by the British as "one of the purest and most exemplary rulers that ever existed," Ahalyā found favour among both Muslims and Hindus and is still revered in Maharashtra.[72]

The most famous vīrāṅganā in North Indian history is also the closest to the present time. In Lakshmībāī, Rānī of Jhansi, is found the summation of the traits already discussed. Born in a Brahmin family from Nagpur, her father Moropant was a military adviser to the exiled Peshwa, and she grew up with Nānā Sāhib and Tāntya Tope, her later allies, in the court at Bithur, learning military skills as well as reading and writing. When she was married to Gangādhar Rāo, the ruler of Jhansi, she brought her father with her. To Gangādhar Rāo, who had been issueless by a previous wife, she produced a son, but he survived only three months. Overcome by grief, Gangādhar Rāo died soon after, although first he made sure to adopt a son as heir. Lakshmībāī took over the affairs of state as regent, and began a series of negotiations with the British to have the adopted son recognized. However, Dalhousie's Doctrine of Lapse was put into effect and Jhansi was annexed by the British in 1857.

During the disturbances that spread over North India in 1857, troops in Jhansi revolted and killed a large number of British citizens. The Rānī's responsibility for this massacre and her relations with the British early in her rule are controversial topics, but it is clear that subsequently she took active leadership in opposing the British suppression of the rebellion. When the British under Hugh Rose marched against her, she defended Jhansi fort and only fled to safety when the British overran the ramparts. She faced the British again in major battles at Kalpi and at Gwalior, where she died in combat.

While the historical details of Lakshmībāī's rule are subjects of debate, in the popular Indian mind she is unequivocally identified as a great freedom fighter in the first stage of India's war of independence against the British. With this are linked a number of heroic images and anecdotes that can now be seen as part of a larger vīrāṅganā complex. Thus, when she was a girl of seven or eight, she tamed an elephant by climbing up its trunk to its tusk.[73] After her marriage, she was stifled by court life and formed a regiment of women, with whom she could practice horseback riding, swordsmanship, pole climbing, and wrestling.[74] It is said that sometimes she fought her enemies with swords in both of her hands and the reins of her horse between her teeth.[75] She was also accomplished at shooting. Most paintings depict her mounted on horseback, carrying a shield in one hand with her sword raised high over her head. Frequently a male child is shown seated behind her or tied to her back in a satchel, a reference to the story of her flight from Jhansi when she "left the fort under cover of darkness on horseback with, as popular tradition has it, her adopted son on her back."[76] Legends abound regarding miraculous feats such as her extraordinary leaps, long and swift rides, and prowess with the sword.

Lakshmībāī's masculine appearance is frequently mentioned as part of her legend. Casting aside the constraints imposed on Brahmin widows, she chose clothing that enabled her to ride and lead a vigorous life. In portraits, she wears either a

Maharashtrian sari draped between the legs, or trousers and a long
tunic belted at the waist, with her sword stuck in the waistband.
At the time of her death, according to Hugh Rose, she was
wearing a red jacket, red trousers, and white turban. Among the
many songs, poems, and novels dealing with her life, perhaps the
best-known is Subhadrā Kumārī Chauhān's paean in Hindi which
uses the refrain *khūb laṟī mardānī vah to jhānsī vālī rānī thī*,
"bravely fought the *mardānī*, the Queen of Jhansi." Here
mardānī signifies a masculine woman, *mardānā* being a Persian
adjective meaning "masculine, valorous," and -ī the feminine
ending in Hindi. John Lang, a British visitor who chanced to
meet her in person, described her physique as that of a strong,
intelligent, dignified individual. Far from being considered odd
or inappropriate, the Rānī's physical presence was extremely
effective in mobilizing her forces to action. Her very arrival on
the battlefield is said to have inspired her troops with courage and
hope.

While Lakshmībāī's fame derives primarily from her
qualities as a warrior, she was also an able administrator, known
for her diligence and sense of justice. Like the queens already
discussed, she acted not only for the protection of her people, but
was also fond of learning, supported the development of the royal
library, provided for the poor, patronized musicians, and
dispensed religious charity. Even her enemies praised her virtues:
"The high descent of the Rani, her unbounded liberality to her
troops and retainers, and her fortitude which no reverses could
shake rendered her an influential and dangerous adversary,"
wrote Sir Hugh Rose.[77]

The evidence presented so far should be sufficient to
indicate the historicity of the *vīrāṅganā* among the major ruling
groups of North India during the last millenium. Additional
examples could be provided from Bengal, Assam, Kashmir, the
South, and the tribal regions. Certain political and personal
circumstances seem to foreshadow the emergence of these queens.
Tutelage and support by a senior male prepared the women for

high office, and the absence or incompetence of adult male heirs often afforded an opportunity to take power. An external threat also appears to have served as a catalyst. Personal inclination and talent were no doubt significant if unchartable factors enabling women to become powerful queens and warriors.

Of equal importance to our study is the enduring place these warrior-women hold in the minds of the people. Their heroic deeds are celebrated in all the vehicles of communication known to the culture, from history books to comics, legends, films, and songs. In these narrative traditions, the vīrāṅganā is often likened to the goddess Durgā or Kālī, particularly during battle. Her iconography links her with the goddess visually, for she carries a sword, as Durgā and Kālī do (sometimes one in each of their many hands), and she rides on her "vehicle," her horse corresponding to Durgā's lion. Her defeat of threatening enemies is comparable to the warring goddesses' punishment of evil demons. The details of folk and popular accounts of historical warrior-queens may indeed be inspired by goddess legends.

And yet the vīrāṅganā overlaps somewhat with the satī, the virtuous female who is truthful, just, and capable of self-sacrifice. Much is made in these stories of the queen's decision to forego self-willed death, implying that greater virtue (sat) resides in serving the country. In several cases, the queens do eventually kill themselves when honour cannot be preserved by any other means. Sat or "truth" in many popular tales of women signifies chastity (also commonly referred to as *pativrat dharm*, see section on folk drama below). However, in the vīrāṅganā accounts, sat is construed somewhat differently. The notable fact is that little or no emphasis is placed on the sexual fidelity of the vīrāṅganā or her status as "wife" or "widow." Here virtue exists without being reduced to the physical purity of the female body; in fact, history preserves the names of several of the warrior-queens' lovers and companions. The vīrāṅganā's status is not defined by her relationship to a man (as wife, mother, or paramour), but by her valorous deeds, and therefore sexual relations cannot impugn her "truth." The startling conjunction of physical prowess, moral strength, and sexual freedom with womanhood in the vīrāṅganā indicates how extraordinary and positively powerful a figure she truly is.

The Vīrāṅganā as Political and Social Symbol

The historical vīrāṅganā as described here owes much to the reconstitution of Indian womanhood that took place in the last century. As mentioned previously, the status of women by the early 1800's had become the site of a moral contest between the colonizers and the colonized. In the arguments made to justify their Empire, the British asserted their right to rule by citing Indian practices like sati, *pardā* (seclusion or veiling of women), and kulinism (hypergamous marriages, especially between very young brides and much older men), which they alleged provided "proof" of the inferior and inhuman treatment of women and the depravity of men. This harsh critique, advanced by a foreign power who had seized economic and military control and now proposed to dismantle an entire societal structure, generated a search for an alternative representation of woman among the Indian elite. As put by Jasodhara Bagchi, "foreign domination and its manifestation of 'progress' brought about the need for an 'order' that had to be located in [the] Hindu past."[78] A counter-discourse emerged through which Indian reformers attempted to show that, whatever the current position, women's status had been high in ancient India.[79] The revalorization of the *sahadharmiṇī*, the wife as companionate participant in religious actions, especially the performance of sacrifices, was one outcome of this search. While redeeming Indian womanhood to an extent, this version conformed largely to the tapasvinī type.

The search for historical models of womanly strength led in another direction as well, toward the vīrāṅganā in the form of the queens, the mothers, the warriors of the past. Much of the impetus here derived from the process of reclaiming martial values set in motion by the colonial confrontation. To overturn British notions of Indians (that is, Indian males) as effeminate and passive, the elite resurrected the "ideology of the martial races," to use Nandy's phrase, rebuilding a more assertive self-image based on the warrior ethic or concept of Kshatriyahood.[80] The new identity of aggressive cultural nationalism valorized those traits informed by Aryan and Kshatriya values, emphasizing vigour and militancy.[81] The immediate project was the construction of an alternative Hindu male, for which examples were sought among specific groups such as Marathas, Rajputs and Sikhs, whom the British had categorized as martial races for army recruitment. These communities were lauded as "heroic," and their past leaders and their victories celebrated widely in popular histories.[82]

Because it was these very groups that worshipped the victorious warrior goddess, the new stress on Kshatriya-style masculinity led oddly to a resurgence of interest in the feminine principle in the cosmos.[83] The conquering female thus became the symbol of a particular stream of Indian nationalism. The vīrāṅganā ideal served not only as a refutation of British allegations of the downtrodden state of Indian womanhood. Much more was conveyed in this heroic model: the vīrāṅganā was the source of emotional and spiritual sustenance, an inspiration to all freedom fighters, men as well as women. Indeed the vīrāṅganā became an emblem of the nation itself (Mother India) engaged in righteous struggle. The images and stories of women-warriors thus acquired a wide range of meanings, a richness of implication that enabled them to serve many new uses.

The crystallization of a womanly heroics of conquest is clear in Bengali novelist Bankimchandra Chatterjee's *Ānandamaṭh* (1882). Central to it is a band of ascetics who are fighting to save India from its Muslim rulers and their British allies. Termed *santān* or "offspring, children," the ascetics worship Krishna but also have a special relationship to Kālī whom they consider the mother of all Hindus and the mother of the country. Inspired by their devotion to Kālī and certain of her aid, the ascetics win a great battle and march through the country chanting Bankim's famous hymn to the mother goddess, "Bande Mātaram."[84] As Bagchi suggests, womanhood in the novel becomes both a symbol of the ravaged order and of the resistance to such ravages.[85] The leading female character, Shānti, plays an active role in the heroic struggle for liberation of the motherland. She dons the male sannyāsin's disguise and fights by the side of her ascetic husband. During the battle, she tackles the British soldiers skillfully, unhorsing Lindley and riding away on his horse. In another novel, Bankim created the female bandit heroine Debī Choudhurānī. Bagchi sees in Shānti and Debī "images of women who have defied the normal canons of femininity." Bankim highlights their vīrāṅganā characteristics to convey the heightened sense of crisis in society, as well as to attempt to resolve it through creating models of resistance.[86]

Another dimension of this process occurred in the field of education. Lala Devraj, the Arya Samaj leader who pioneered women's higher education in the Punjab, created a new curriculum for women that included a model of Indian womanhood conforming to the vīrāṅganā type. While writing textbooks, he emphasized courageous European women's lives and created Indian heroines, such as Suvritā and the near-mythic Surī Suvīrā who manifested the heroic virtues. In his women's college, a game called Suvīrā was played "about a warrior girl who is not only brave in defence of her rights but can also wield modern weapons."[87] Other fictional materials used in the classroom dealt with themes like "Ek Rāt" (One Night), which describes a brave young girl who fights singlehandedly with four burglars while her brother is terrified. Through these role models, educationists presented girls with the possibility of new career alternatives, including the option of "becoming not only the pride but also the saviours of the nation."[88] The reinforcement of a strong, positive female identity through the invocation of historically prominent women continues in practices such as naming hostels after famous queens, philosophers, and poets.[89]   As women's higher education continues to be largely segregated from that of men throughout South Asia, the possibilities for preserving women's history and lore would appear to be greater than in the Western education system, where male-centered interpretations of history and culture have dominated for centuries and are only slowly being challenged by feminist scholars.

In the political ideologies that arose in pre-Independence India, it can generally be said that while women's issues were rarely neglected, the more conservative view favored a passive, self-sacrificing posture for womanhood, while the more radical position embraced the activist vīrāṅganā ideal.   Mahatma Gandhi, committed as he was to non-violence and passive resistance, saw the epic heroines Sītā and Sāvitrī as the ideal embodiments of his political strategy. He believed women were by nature non-violent, and therefore they could and should play a major role in the nationalist movement. Gandhi emulated the virtue of taking suffering upon oneself, as a purificatory path to spiritual power, and insofar as women were "the embodiment of sacrifice, silent suffering, humility, faith and knowledge," they were the most effective and reliable force for his non-cooperation campaigns.[90] Thus, even as he brought women out of seclusion and into the streets, Gandhi together with Sarojini Naidu and other followers redefined the passive heroism of the traditional woman in positive terms, in contrast to the bolder models of female achievement and bravery filling the new Arya Samaj classrooms.[91]

Perhaps, as some have suggested, Gandhi's Sītā was not so passive after all.[92] There is no doubt however that his concept of *ahimsā* (non-violence) was in opposition to the vīrāṅganā's direct appropriation of force in defence of honour and justice. India's first Prime Minister, Jawaharlal Nehru, evinced more suspicion toward Sītā and Sāvitrī as role models. In a speech in 1928 he said, "We hear a good deal about Sītā and

Sāvitrī. They are revered names in India and rightly so, but I have a feeling that these echoes from the past are raised chiefly to hide our present deficiencies and to prevent us from attacking the root cause of women's degradation in India today."[93] For Nehru, that root cause was economic bondage, which could be alleviated only when women went to work outside the home and became economically independent.

The symbolism of the vīrānganā was eagerly seized upon by the proponents of revolutionary nationalism, chiefly Bal Gangadhar Tilak and his heirs, who favored the use of force in defeating the British. For this group and their many sympath- izers, the Rānī of Jhansi became a byword for resistance to the British, and was the subject of many clandestine literary works.[94] In 1911 during Ramlila celebrations in U.P., pictures of the Rānī appeared together with Aurobindo Ghosh, Tilak, and Lala Lajpat Rai, establishing the association that the British wished so vigilantly to suppress.[95] During World War II, when Netaji Subhash Chandra Bose reconstituted his Indian National Army in Southeast Asia, he created a women's regiment and named it after the Rānī of Jhansi. Over fifteen hundred women joined under the command of Lakshmi Swaminathan, who is now an organizer in the Communist Party of India-Marxist.[96] The vīrānganā's exemplary valour seemed to be coupled here with a notion of female solidarity that has become more common of late. Feminist groups are now claiming the Rānī of Jhansi, while at the same time, the Congress-I has reportedly depicted Indira Gandhi in a film as a reincarnation of the Rānī, dressed like her with sword and shield.

Vīrānganās in Hindi Folk Drama

Complementing and intersecting the historical vīrānganā is the vīrānganā of contemporary folklore and legend. The sources analyzed in this section all belong to the folk theatre genre known as *nauṭaṅkī*, or in earlier parlance, *svāṅg*, *sāṅg*, or *sāṅgīt*. Nauṭaṅkī texts have been printed by popular publishers in the Hindi-speaking region since the mid-1800's, and they provide an unparalleled resource for analyzing the outlook of the ordinary people. These texts (or more accurately libretti) form the basis of entertainment-oriented performances, played by itinerant troupes at fairs, festivals, or weddings. Textual portions are sung to fixed musical patterns, accompanied by the loud *naggārā* (kettledrums) and a melodic instrument such as harmonium, *shehnāī*, *sāraṅgī*, or flute. Performances may also include clowning sequences, erotic dancing, acrobatics, or topical skits. Stories are drawn from Hindu and Islamic romances, local legends, tales of saints, even newspaper accounts and recently film plots.

In the nineteenth century, women did not appear on the Nauṭaṅkī stage, and female roles were enacted by men, but beginning in the 1920's and 30's, women began to sing and play parts, and in the latest phase of development, they own and operate some of the major Nauṭaṅkī companies. The position of women in this theatre is made more complex by the negative moral associations of Nauṭaṅkī-viewing for the high castes. Women have often been prevented from attending Nauṭaṅkī shows, which have evolved in such a way as to cater to male interest in sexual display and innuendo. Nonetheless, the traditional stories of Nauṭaṅkī often show women in strong warlike stances. This section will demonstrate the operation of the vīrāṅganā ideal among female protagonists in the Nauṭaṅkī folk theatre.

One of the earliest stories in the Nauṭaṅkī repertoire is *Syāhposh*, or as it was called in the nineteenth century, *Saudāgar o Syāhposh*. This is the tale of a merchant's son, Gabrū, who attempts to win the hand of Jamāl, the daughter of a minister of state, after being enchanted by hearing her reading from the *Qurān*. While visiting Jamāl, Gabrū is apprehended one night by the king, disguised as a police constable roaming the city to ensure its safety. Gabrū is sentenced to hang, and at the scene of the gallows, he waits anxiously for a last vision of his beloved. Jamāl finally appears dressed as a man all in black (*syāh posh*), riding a horse, wielding a dagger and a sword. She threatens to commit suicide by stabbing herself or drinking a cup of poison. The king is persuaded of the true love of the couple and marries them on the spot.

Similar tales of dangerous love between a highly ranked valorous woman and a commoner male abound in the Nauṭaṅkī literature. In *Shīrīn Farhād*, the stonecutter Farhād falls in love with queen Shīrīn while engaged in building a canal for her. Later he is given the task of digging a tunnel through an impenetrable mountain, and while he is working Shīrīn rides out on horseback to meet him for a rendezvous. *Lākhā Bañjārā* relates the love between a princess and Lākhā, the son of a trader. Similar to *Syāhposh* in many details, it culminates in Lākhā's being arrested by a policeman while returning from the princess one night, followed by a death-sentence by the king, and the appearance of the princess at the gallows pleading with her father for her lover's release. However, in this story the king does not relent, Lākhā is killed, and the lovers are united only after Guru Gorakhnāth arrives and resuscitates Lākhā.

Perhaps the most striking instance is the story of *Nauṭaṅkī Shāhzādī*, "The Princess Nauṭaṅkī," whose name came to signify this theatre genre. "Nauṭaṅkī" means a woman whose weight is nine *ṭaṅk*s (a ṭaṅk equals four grams), implying that she was very delicate (at least in the beginning of the story). Phūl Singh sets out in quest of her following a dare from his sister-in-law, travelling from Punjab to Multan and finally gaining entrance to her private garden. There he courts her but their love is discovered during the ritual weighing that occurs every day to test Nauṭaṅkī's chastity. Sentenced by the king to hang, Phūl Singh awaits his execution when suddenly Nauṭaṅkī arrives at the gallows, dressed as a man and armed with sword and dagger. Phūl Singh is content with this last glimpse of her, and he bids farewell to the world as the noose is placed around his neck. But Nautaṅkī pulls out a cup of poison and prepares to commit suicide, vowing to die like Shīrīn died for Farhād and Lailā for Majnūn. As the executioners advance to pull the cord, she rushes with her dagger and drives them off. She then turns her sword on her father, demanding he pardon her lover at once. The king consents to the marriage and the two are wedded at once.

Although details differ, these stories all involve a romantic quest by a lover (usually a social inferior) for a princess. The quest is fraught with danger, expressed not only in the lover's travails in reaching the princess and obtaining her consent, but in the punishment meted out for violation of her honour. In each case, the princess becomes her lover's rescuer in the end. She braves social censure, daring to leave the seclusion of her palace and appear in public, thus demonstrating the great measure of her love. She also challenges the chief representative of society's moral order, the king or her father (frequently one and the same), by pleading for permission to marry and even threatening his life. To carry out her brave resolve, she transforms herself into a warrior figure, attired as a soldier on a horse carrying weapons. In these cases, then, the vīrāṅganā shares some of the characteristics of the historical queens, including the male costume, position on horseback, and protective use of sword and dagger. Her cause, however, is not defence of the homeland but salvation of her lover and achievement of ultimate union with him. She appears only as a vīrāṅganā when her lover is mortally threatened, although her social superiority to the male invests her with power throughout the story.

The queenly type of vīrāṅganā known to history has also been made the subject of Nautaṅkī plays. Three plays with the title Sāṅgīt Mahārānī Tārā (presumably the Tārābāī discussed earlier) appear in the catalogues of the British Museum and the India Office Library. Two plays exist on Mahārānī Durgāvatī, but the one in my collection appears to be quite a different story from that of Durgāvatī of Gondwana.

The most popular vīrāṅganā story in the Nauṭaṅkī world appears to be *Vīrāṅganā Vīrmatī*. Vīrmatī and her husband Jagdev's tale was first recorded in dramatic form in 1876, but it reached prominence in the 1920's when the two most commonly performed versions of it were published, those of Shrikrishna Khatri of the Kanpur style of Nauṭaṅkī and of Natharam Sharma Gaur of the Hathras style.[97] The present discussion follows Natharam's text.

King Udiyaditya of Malwa has two wives, Baghelin and Solankin. Baghelin's son is a coward, while Jagdev, son of Solankin, is brave and virtuous and his father's favourite. Baghelin fears that Jagdev may soon become king, and she forces the king to insult Jagdev by asking him to return the horse and swords he had presented to him previously. As a result, Jagdev leaves the court followed by his wife Vīrmatī, who vows to be at his side no matter what difficulties lie ahead. After wandering for some time, they reach a lake, and Jagdev leaves his wife while he goes to find lodging in the nearby city. Vīrmatī is then approached by a prostitute and enticed to the brothel of Jāmoti, on the pretext that Jāmoti is her husband's sister.

So far the events bear an uncanny resemblance to the *Rāmāyaṇa*: the rivalry between co-wives to determine whose son shall be heir, the exit of the favoured son, accompanied by his devoted wife, the wife's abandonment in the hostile forest and her abduction. At this point in the Nauṭaṅkī however, Vīrmatī's similarity to the passive, patient Sītā ends. Lāljī, son of the Kotwal, tries to seduce Vīrmatī, but she gets him drunk and then kills him with his own sword. She dumps the body from the window, and when the Kotwal discovers his dead son, he rushes in to the brothel to arrest her. However, Vīrmatī, still holding the Kotwal's sword, proceeds to kill twenty-five of the Kotwal's men. Jagdev eventually finds Vīrmatī, and the couple are welcomed by the king of the city. In this episode, Vīrmatī's bravery is explicitly directed toward protecting her chastity (pativrat dharm). In the text, she is compared to a lioness (*shernī*) with bloodshot eyes and a fierce roar. She is also likened to Kālī dancing on the chest of her victims.[98]

In the second part of the story, Vīrmatī proves herself capable of even greater courage when she beheads her own husband. Jagdev was tricked by the goddess Kankālī (also called Kālikā, both variants of Kālī) into giving her his head, which she demanded as a religious gift (*dān*), in retribution for his assault on her son, the demon Kaluā. Vīrmatī impresses even the blood-thirsty Kankālī with her tearless fulfillment of duty, and eventually Kankālī joins Jagdev's head back to his body and revives him. Through this test, Vīrmatī proves herself to be a true daughter of the goddess, and Kankālī addresses her as such while Vīrmatī in return addresses Kankālī as mother. In the end, Jagdev and Vīrmatī return home, where Baghelin has repented, and they all live happily.

In the vīrānganās in Nautankī, we see a shift from the brave acts of the historical queens in defence of their homeland, to brave deeds aimed at the preservation of a woman's family honour and sexual purity. The two are closely related; if a woman is married to a king, her chastity constitutes the essence of family honour, in turn equated with the honour of the kingdom. The fundamental point of comparison is that in both cases women are fighting actively, moving on their own initiative and strength to protect themselves and gain their own victories. The imagery of the vīrānganā is also remarkably consistent, with repeated mention of the woman riding on horseback, armed with sword and dagger.

The Cinema Claims the Vīrānganā

The early Indian cinema in many ways transported the folk theatre of the late 19th and early 20th centuries into the celluloid medium. The singers and actors from the theatre found new jobs for themselves in the film industry, and many of the former theatre managers and commercial backers joined to form film companies. The stories used in the first twenty or so years of Indian cinema repeated the popular plots from the Nauṭaṅkī, Tamāshā, and Pārsī theatres, which had earlier inherited them from all-India and regional sources. As Pradip Kishen has noted, "that the cinema actively set out to displace folk entertainments is suggested by the fact that the cinema appropriated its forms, transposing its ingredients and often its subjects, into the standard fare of the Indian screen."[99]

Given these continuities, it is not surprising to find a veritable spate of films in the twenties, thirties, and forties devoted to the vīrāṅganā type. Among the silent movies of the twenties, the following were based on specific women-warriors discussed above: *Sati Veermat* (1921), *Devi Ahalyabai* (1925), and *Sultana Chandbibi* (1932); talking versions were later released of *Tara Sundari* (1934), *Sultana Chand Bibi* (1936), *Taramati* (1945), as well as several films on other Rajput heroines like Padmini, Pannadai, and Minaldevi. There were also a number of films dealing with less historical and occasionally more fanciful vīrāṅganās. In the silent category, these included: *A Fair Warrior* (1927), *Veerangana* (1928), *Female Feat* (1929), *Chatur Sundari* (Wily Heroine), *Goddess of War* (Ran Chandi, based on Puranic mythology, 1930), *Shurvir Sharda* (Gallant Girl, 1930), *Valiant Princess* (1930), *Lionness* (1931), *Valiant Angel* (Chitod ki Veerangana, 1931), *Stree Shakti* (The Super Sex, 1932), *Daring Damsel* (Azad Abla, 1933), *The Amazon* (Dilruba Daku, 1933), and *The Lady Cavalier* (Ratna Lutari, 1933). Among the sound pictures, similar titles abound: *Veer Kumari* (1935), *Jungle Queen* (1936), *Chabukwali* (1938), *Aflatoon Aurat* (Amazon, 1940), *Veerangana* (1947), and so on.[100]

Worthy of special mention are the films that starred the actress Nadia: *Hunterwali* (1934), *Sher Dil*, *Lutaru Lalna* (1938), *Diamond Queen* (1940), and many others. These films, directed mostly by Homi Wadia, were extremely popular in the thirties and forties, and were part of the childhood experience of many of the actors and directors of today, as Girish Karnad recalls:

> The single most memorable sound of my child-hood is the clarion call of 'Hey-y-y-y-y-' as Fearless Nadia, regal on her horse, her hand raised defiantly in the air, rode down upon the bad guys. To us school kids of the mid-40's Fearless Nadia meant courage, strength, idealism.[101]

In these films, Nadia played the valiant heroine who always comes to the rescue, her most frequent entrance, as recounted here, being on horseback. Stills from her films show her carrying every conceivable kind of weapon — bow and arrow, sword, bullwhip, and pistol — as well as lifting men over her head and throwing them.

The theatrical origins of Nadia's role are suggested in the following excerpt, which seems to describe the *Syāhposh* type of vīrāṅganā discussed above:

> The good king was imprisoned by the scheming minister. The righteous among the subjects were tortured or locked up. The helpless princess, driven to despair, unable to find succor finally decided to act on her own and set things right. And in a moment, the large fair woman, whose discomfort seemed to arise more from the sari she was wrapped in than from the political situation, transformed herself into a masked woman, in tight black costume, who could ride, swim, fight, wrestle, fence and even take a reverse jump from ground to balcony.[102]

The Nadia/Wadia productions, beginning with *Hunterwali* (The Lady with the Whip), created a new genre, the stunt film, but without the luxuries of stunt directors, duplicate stuntmen, and the trick photography of today. The famous train films like *Frontier Mail* (1936) also originated at this time, with Nadia performing daring feats on the top of moving trains. These popular genres eventually gave way to the "socials," family dramas involving more "realistic" situations, although current films still incorporate noticeable vīrāṅganā elements.

Prior to Independence in 1947, films suggesting nationalist messages were strictly censored. It is significant that not one film on the list above appears with the Rānī of Jhansi, the most famous vīrāṅganā, as its heroine. The Rānī was simply too potent a nationalist symbol to be allowed on the screen. Articles, poems, plays, even the noted Hindi novel by Vrindāvan Lāl Vermā on the Rānī of Jhansi were immediately banned upon publication.[103] In the absence of such obvious nationalist images, it is likely that the semiotic value of figures like Fearless Nadia and other cinematic vīrāṅganās owed much to their patriotic implications. The vīrāṅganā story was a convenient, popularly understood allegory used to circumvent restrictions on explicit political content.

This is not to deny the obvious entertainment value that the vīrāṅganā came to possess in the process of becoming a cinematic image. The wonderment and reverence associated with the earlier legends of valiant women now acquired a cruder colouring as heroic feats were converted into "stunts," and the female body was displayed in erotically charged, athletic poses. Nonetheless the cinematic vīrāṅganā emerging in this period indicates the full assimilation of the paradigm into the popular culture of the twentieth century.

Low Caste Heroines: Phūlan Devī and the Bandit Queens

The most recent manifestation of this heroic mode is the female outlaw figure, counterpart to the Robin Hood-like male dacoit (*ḍākū*), a common subject of North Indian folklore. Just as the ḍākū is considered a Rājā or king by his followers and the villagers within his territory, so too the "bandit queen" shares the symbolic character of sovereignty with the historical queens discussed above. She is a woman of indomitable courage, a merciless executrix of justice. Adored by her people both for her beauty and her power, she leads her gang, utilizing the same weapons and costume as her male cohorts. Former vīrāṅganās defended their kingdoms and fought enemies of opposing ethnic and religious composition; the female outlaw fights the police, landlords, and the wealthy, and she defends the rights of the poor and oppressed. Since the 1960's and 70's, she is increasingly a low-caste heroine in alliance with the disprivileged in rural society, in opposition to Brahmins, Ṭhākurs, and government officials.

The female outlaw as a sub-type of the vīrāṅganā appeared in several films of the thirties, e.g. *Lady Robinhood*, *The Amazon* (*Dilruba Daku*), and *Lady Cavalier* (*Ratna Lutari*). Numerous legends grew up around Putlī Bāī, a famous one-armed dacoit of the fifties, celebrating her exploits in the Chambal Valley.[104] But the most widely publicized story has been that of Phūlan Devī, whose recent career has been featured in international magazines like *Time* and *Esquire* on the one hand, and who on the other hand has inspired folk poets to compose *nauṭaṅkī*s, *bārahmāsī*s, *birahā*s, and other folklore genres in Hindi dialects. Several Hindi films have been produced about her, including the rather faithful version of her life, *Kahānī Phūlvatī kī*.[105] Clay idols of her have been sold together with other gods and goddesses in the local markets.[106] Her example has made such an impact that many other women of her region have become dacoits.[107] By 1986 bandit gangs considered it *de rigueur* to have at least one female member.[108]

Prior to her arrest in 1983 Phulan had become a media phenomenon, the object of sensationalistic exaggeration and romanticization nourished by lack of concrete information. Since

the release of photographs taken at her surrender and the publication of various interviews conducted in jail, the fantastic rumours
about her beauty and charm have been put to rest, and the myth
has been partially dismantled. Nonetheless it is a measure of the
meaningfulness of Phūlan's story that it continues to be an
oft-told one, and that in its essential details there is little variance
between the many types of sources, be they folk poems or
journalistic accounts.[109] The following synopsis is a composite
of elements drawn from folk and media sources.

Phūlan was born a Mallāh (boatman subcaste) in 1956 in
a village in Jalaun District, U.P. The chain of exploitation that
characterizes her life began with her marriage at the age of ten to
a lustful widower twenty years her senior. When she escaped
from his advances and returned to her village, the panchayat
expelled her, and she went to live with an uncle whose sons and
friends harassed her. According to some folk accounts, she then
met a dacoit named Kailāsh and married him in court but was
later offered to his friend Vikram (another Mallāh) and the gang
leader Bābū Gūjar for their sexual enjoyment. She was arrested
on a robbery charge and spent three weeks in police custody
where she was sexually assaulted. Released through the good
graces of a Ṭhākur, he afterwards forced her to become his
concubine. Kailāsh meanwhile was killed by the police, and
Phūlan came under Vikram's protection. After killing Bābū
Gūjar, Vikram established himself as a gang leader with Phūlan
as his mistress. He taught her to shoot, and the two began a series
of robberies and murders in the Chambal region. Internal feuding
in the gang led to Vikram being killed by Srīrām and Lālārām,
two Ṭhākur gang members. They kidnapped Phūlan Devī, took
her to Behmai village, and kept her captive while she was raped
by a number of other Ṭhākur men for several days. Beaten and
humiliated, she was forced to draw water from the village and
serve the men. This incident fueled Phūlan's final revenge.
After escaping from Behmai, she joined with another dacoit,
Mustaqīm and returned with his gang to Behmai to avenge the

murder of Vikram and repay the Ṭhākurs for dishonouring her. She lined up twenty Ṭhākur men and massacred them on Valentine's Day, 1981. After evading police pursuit for two years, she was finally sent to jail in Madhya Pradesh following a negotiated surrender with the police.

The central theme of Phūlan's life as interpreted by popular opinion is one of repeated victimization, particularly sexual assault by men, leading eventually to resistance and counterattack upon the perpetrators. Phūlan was robbed and looted of her chastity ("to rape" in Hindi is *izzat lūtnā*, "to steal one's honour"), and so she turns to robbing and looting in return. Her struggle has much to do with the oppressive caste system of rural North India. As a low-caste woman, she was raped many times by high-caste men, and it is towards them that she directs her avenging fury. As she states in the Nauṭaṅkī play *Phūlan Debī*: "Ṭhākurs have done whatever they wanted with me. High-caste men always played with my honour. Not until I shoot them each one by one will their oppression of me be repaid."[110] Becoming a bandit, she dressed in the khaki uniform of a senior superintendent of police, tied a headband around her cropped hair, donned running shoes, and toted a rifle — a modern-day equivalent to the turbaned, sword-wielding historical vīrāṅganā on horseback. In defending her honour, and that of all low-caste women, Phūlan is a woman-warrior who secures the triumph of the sexually and economically exploited. She continues the noble tradition of valiant women who protect themselves and others through their own courageous albeit bloody deeds.

In the masculinist press, Phūlan has been portrayed as an irresistible, insatiable man-eater. The image constructed of her combines elements of wild beauty, seductiveness, and extraordinary danger. *Esquire* describes her as "a legendary six-foot-tall, raven-haired, one-armed beauty," "a beautiful femme fatale who had butchered twice as many men as she had bedded."[111] There is no doubt that a genuine terror of her (as of dacoits in general) existed in the countryside in the months following the

Behmai massacre and preceding her capture. However, it is noteworthy that Phūlan has also become a symbol of women's liberation, to urban Indians as well as to the rural women who emulate her. Phūlan and her sister-bandits, Kusuma Nain, Meera Thakur, and others, have been called a "beacon of hope for countless young women who have a score to settle with society."[112] In Bombay and Delhi, Phūlan "appeared to represent the ideas expressed by such feminists as Kate Millett, Betty Friedan, and Germaine Greer," in her stance as "the new woman ... a brash Amazon who had risen above her caste and the traditionally subservient position of the Indian female."[113]

Phūlan achieved prominence in an era in which more and more women were emerging from their domestic seclusion and taking up positions side by side with men in schools and colleges, in the workplace, in politics and public life. Her powerful presence has quickened awareness about the changes that await both women and men in the years to come. For some she has heightened anxieties about the current transformation underway in women's roles, while for others she has come to inspire determined commitment to the struggle for equality and justice for women. In Phūlan, the contemporary incarnation of the vīrāṅganā lives on.

Notes

1. My reference is primarily to Bharata's *Nātyaśāstra*, the first of the great exegeses of dramaturgy and poetics, composed around the 2nd century B.C. Later aestheticians specify nine moods.

2. Kumkum Sangari and Sudesh Vaid, "Reflections on Women and Culture," in Kumkum Sangari and Sudesh Vaid, eds., *Women and Culture* (Bombay: SNDT Women's University, Research Centre for Women's Studies, 1985), 1.

3. Andrea Dworkin, *Woman Hating* (New York: E.P. Dutton, 1974), 42.

4. Madhu Kishwar and Ruth Vanita, eds., *In Search of Answers: Indian Women's Voices from Manushi* (London: Zed Books Ltd., 1984), 46.

5. Katherine K. Young, "Hinduism," in Arvind Sharma, ed., *Women in World Religions* (Albany: State University of New York Press, 1987), 75.

6. Young, "Hinduism," 73.

7. Young, "Hinduism," 69.

8. The ideal may be far from the reality as experienced by many women. The account of Doranne Jacobson's inform-ant Bhuri, a Brahmin village woman from Madhya Pradesh, suggests that the "chaste wife" norm is observed more in the breach than the practice. Doranne Jacobson, "The Chaste Wife: Cultural Norm and Individual Experience," in Sylavia Vatuk, ed., *American Studies in the Anthropology of India* (New Delhi: Manohar Publications, 1978), 94-138.

9. Julia Leslie, "Suttee or *Sati*: Victim or Victor?" in Julia Leslie, ed., *Roles and Rituals for Hindu Women* (London: Pinter Publishers, 1991), 187.

10. I. Julia Leslie, *The Perfect Wife: The Orthodox Hindu Woman according to the Strīdharmapaddhati of Tryambakayajvan* (Delhi: Oxford University Press, 1989), 321.

11. Hank Heifetz, trans., *The Origin of the Young God: Kālidāsa's Kumārasambhava* (Berkeley: University of California Press, 1985), 67.

54   Kathryn Hansen

12. Heifetz, 70-71.

13. Heifetz, 81.

14. David Kinsley, *Hindu Goddesses* (Berkeley: University of California Press, 1986), 53.

15. Kinsley, *Goddesses*, 54.

16. Uma Chakravarti, "The Development of the Sita Myth: A Case Study of Women in Myth and Literature," in *Women and Culture*, 62-63.

17. Brenda E.F. Beck, "Fate, Karma, and Cursing in a Local Epic Milieu," in Charles F. Keyes and E. Valentine Daniel, eds., *Karma: An Anthropological Inquiry* (Berkeley: University of California Press, 1983), 78.

18. Brenda E.F. Beck, *The Three Twins: The Telling of a South Indian Folk Epic* (Bloomington: Indiana University Press, 1982), 156-157.

19. Veena Das, "The Mythological Film and its Framework of Meaning: An Analysis of *Jai Santoshi Ma*," *India International Centre Quarterly*, 8:1 (March 1980), 48.

20. Susan S. Wadley, "*Vrats:* Transformers of Destiny," in *Karma*, 148.

21. Mary McGee, "Desired Fruits: Motive and Intention in the Votive Rites of Hindu Women," in *Roles and Rituals*, 71.

22. McGee, 74.

23. McGee, 79-80.

24. Shudha Mazumdar, *Memoirs of an Indian Woman*, ed. Geraldine Forbes (New York: M.E. Sharpe, 1989), 23.

25. Mazumdar, 24.

26. Lynn Bennett, *Dangerous Wives and Sacred Sisters* (New York: Columbia University Press, 1983), 47.

27. Bennett, 61.

28. Bennett, 176.

29. Bennett, 45.

30. Bennett, 176.

31. Bennett, 176-177.

32. McGee, 84.

33. In the section that follows, the English-language reader may not notice that two related but distinct Sanskrit terms are being employed. Sati (without any diacritical mark) refers to the act, while satī (with a long "ī") refers to the women. This discussion is restricted to placing sati in an ideological perspective, trying to understand its *raison d'être*, rather than examining its definition, practice, reform and so on from a sociohistorical perspective, a task that others have already attempted. See, for example, two recent additions to the literature: Sakuntala Narasimhan, *Sati: A Study of Widow Burning in India* (Delhi: Viking, 1990), and Arvind Sharma, *et. al.*, *Sati: Historical and Phenomenological Essays* (Delhi: Motilal Banarsidass, 1988).

34. Kinsley, *Goddesses*, 37.

35. Kinsley, *Goddesses*, 41.

36. Kumkum Sangari and Sudesh Vaid, "Sati in Modern India, A Report," in *Women and Culture*, 256-257.

37. Sangari and Vaid, "Sati," 259.

38. For scholars such as Lata Mani, sati cannot be contextualized without examining the colonial intervention, missionary discourse, and reformist thinkers such as Ram Mohan Roy. Lata Mani, "Contentious Traditions: The Debate on *Sati* in Colonial India," in Kumkum Sangari and Sudesh Vaid, eds., *Recasting Women: Essays in Colonial History* (Delhi: Kali for Women, 1989), 88-126.

39. Uma Chakravarti, "Whatever Happened to the Vedic *Dāsī?*" in *Recasting Women: Essays in Colonial History*, 28.

40. Chakravarti, "Whatever Happened?", 51-52.

41. O.P. Kejariwal, *The Asiatic Society of Bengal and the Discovery of India's Past* (Delhi: Oxford University Press, 1988), 76.

42. Chakravarti, "Whatever Happened?", 31.

43. Chakravarti, "Whatever Happened", 44.

44. Katherine Young, "From Hindu Strīdharma to Universal Feminism: A Study of the Women of the Nehru Family," in Peter Slater and Donald Wiebe, eds., *Traditions in Contact and Change* (Waterloo: Wilfrid Laurier University Press, 1983), 92.

45. Ashish Nandy, *The Intimate Enemy: Loss and Recovery of Self Under Colonialism* (Delhi: Oxford University Press, 1988), 4.

46. Nandy, 52-53.

47. Young, "From Strīdharma," 92.

48. "I would love to find that my future army contained a vast preponderance of women over men. If the fight came, I should then approach it with much greater confidence than if men predominated. I would dread the latter's violence. Women would be my guarantee against such an outbreak." M.K. Gandhi, *Women and Social Injustice* (1942), quoted in Patricia Caplan, *Class and Gender in India* (London: Tavistock Publications, 1985), 114.

49. Kinsley, *Goddesses*, 30.

50. Kinsley, *Goddesses*, 95.

51. Kinsley, *Goddesses*, 97.

52. A list of 51 epithets for the Devī from the *Devī-Mahātmya* is discussed in Thomas B. Coburn, *Devī Mahātmya: The Crystallization of the Goddess Tradition* (Delhi: Motilal Banarsidass, 1984), 89-208.

53. David R. Kinsley, "Blood and Death Out of Place: Reflections on the Goddess Kali," in John Stratton Hawley and Donna Marie Wulff, eds., *The Divine Consort: Radha and the Goddesses of India* (Boston: Beacon Press, 1982), 145.

54. Kinsley, *Goddesses*, 107.

55. Kinsley, *Goddesses*, 109-110.

56. Bennett, 138-141.

57. Kinsley, *Goddesses*, 202-203.

58. David D. Shulman, "Battle as Metaphor in Tamil Folk and Classical Traditions," in Stuart H. Blackburn and A.K. Ramanujan, eds., *Another Harmony: New Essays on the Folklore of India* (Berkeley: University of California Press, 1986), 107-113.

59. John J. Pool, *Famous Women in India* (Calcutta: Susil Gupta Ltd., 1954), 86.

60. Swami Madhavananda and Ramesh Chandra Majumdar, eds., *Great Women of India* (Almora: Advaita Ashrama, 1953), 321; also James Tod, *Annals and Antiquities of Rajasthan* (London: George Routledge and Sons Ltd., 1914), Vol. 1, 211.

61. The Amar Chitra Katha version notes that she first intended to become a satī but decided to raise her son instead. Prakash Khanna, trans., *Rānī Durgāvatī* (Bombay: India Book House, reprinted 1984), 4.

62. Abul Fazl, cited in Madhavananda, 323-324.

63. Madhavananda, 324.

64. Cited in Madhavananda, 324.

65. Madhavananda, 392.

66. Pool, 143-4.

67. Tod, 237.

68. Madhavananda, 359; see also Amar Chitra Katha comic by Meena Ranade, *Ahilyabai Holkar* (Bombay: India Book House, n.d.), 5-6.

3

69. In the Amar Chitra Katha version, Ahalya wavers between the selfish performance of sati, for her own salvation, and the decision to dedicate her life to the service of others; Ranade, 12-13.

70. John Malcolm, *A Memoir of Central India, including Malwa*, (London: Parbury, Allen and Co., 1982), Vol. 1, 162.

71. Malcolm, 179.

72. Malcolm, 194.

73. Joyce Lebra-Chapman, *The Rani of Jhansi: A Study of Female Heroism in India* (Honolulu: University of Hawaii Press, 1986), 16.

74. Lebra-Chapman, 19, 22.

75. Shyam Narain Sinha, *Rani Lakshmi Bai of Jhansi* (Allahabad: Chugh Publications, 1980), 97.

76. Lebra-Chapman, 93.

77. Sinha, 97.

78. Jasodhara Bagchi, "Positivism and Nationalism: Womanhood and Crisis in Nationalist Fiction," in *Economic and Political Weekly*, 20:43, WS-60.

79. Kumari Jayawardena, *Feminism and Nationalism in the Third World* (London: Zed Books Ltd.), 78.

80. Nandy, 7.

81. Chakravarti, "Whatever Happened?", 49.

82. Chakravarti, "Whatever Happened," 47-48.

83. Nandy, 10.

84. A modern translation of the work appears to be lacking; however for a Victorian version, see *The Abbey of Bliss*, translated by Nares Chandra Sen-Gupta (Calcutta: The Cherry Press, 1900); the hymn first occurs on 32-33. It had been composed earlier by Bankim, and some twenty years later was adopted as the anthem of the Swadeshi movement. This latter topic was taken up in Rabindranath Tagore's novel *Ghare Baire* (The Home and the World) and beautifully handled by Satyajit Ray in his film of the same title.

85. Bagchi, WS-61.

86. Bagchi, WS-61.

87. Madhu Kishwar, "Arya Samaj and Women's Education," in *Economic and Political Weekly*, 21:17, WS-13.

88. Kishwar, "Arya Samaj," 17.

89. Conversation with Tara Sinha.

90. Jayawardena, 95-97.

91. For Sarojini Naidu's role in invoking the epic heroines, see Lou Ratte, "Goddesses, Mothers, and Heroines: Hindu Women and the Feminine in the Early Nationalist Movement," in Yvonne Yazbeck Haddad, ed., *Women, Religion and Social Change* (Albany: State University of New York Press, 1985), 367-370.

92. Kishwar, *In Search*, 47.

93. Jayawardena, 98.

94. Lebra-Chapman, 143-146.

95. Sandria B. Freitag, *Collective Action and Community: Public Arenas and the Emergence of Communalism in North India* (Berkeley: University of California Press, 1989), 202-203.

96. Lebra-Chapman, 150.

97. Other narrative versions of it are contained in Richard Carnac Temple, *The Legends of the Panjab* (Patiala: Language Department, Punjab, 1962 [first pub. 1884]), Vol. 2, 182-203, and Anil Rajkumar, *Bhāratīya vīrānganāen* (Delhi: Kitab Ghar, 1984), 58-71.

98. Natharam Sharma Gaur, *Sāngīt Vīrānganā Vīrmatī* (Hathras: Shyam Press, 1971), Vol. 1, 42-43.

99. Pradip Kishen, introducing an interview article with Komal Kothari, "Myths, Tales and Folklore: Exploring the Substratum of Cinema," *India International Centre Quarterly*, 8:1, 31.

100. Information drawn from Firoze Rangoonwalla, *Indian Filmography: Silent and Hindi Films (1897-1969)* (Bombay: J. Udeshi, 1970).

101. Girish Karnad, "This One is for Nadia," *Cinema Vision India*, 1:2, 86.

102. Karnad, 85.

103. Lebra-Chapman, 146.

104. Taroon Coomar Bhaduri, *Chambal: The Valley of Terror* (Delhi: Vikas Publishing House, 1972), 54-66.

105. Conversation with Alan Entwistle.

106. "Phoolan fever," *Times of India*, October 24, 1984, 1.

107. Sunil Saxena, "The Bullet Queens," *Times of India*, Aug. 18, 1985, 3.

108. "Return to Dacoity," *India Today*, Oct. 31, 1986, 33.

109. The most recent major publication to my knowledge is Mala Sen, *India's Bandit Queen: The True Story of Phoolan Devi* (Delhi: Indus, 1991).

110. Svaminath, *Sāṅgīt Phūlan Debī* (Ayodhya: Ramlakhan Gupta Bookseller, 1982), 46.

111. Jon Bradshaw, "The Bandit Queen," *Esquire*, October 1985, 73.

112. *Times of India*, Aug. 18, 1985.

113. Bradshaw, 86.

MOTHER INDIA, MOTHER GODDESS AND MILITANCY IN NEO-HINDUISM: THE ROLE OF SISTER NIVEDITĀ

Nalini Devdas

Thou Naked Sword of Purity!
Thou, that cleavest all bondage,
Thou, Destroyer of Ignorance,
Thou, Refuser of attachments,
Thou, that remainest ever Thyself
To Thee our salutation![1]

This verse of devotion to Goddess Kālī the Mother was written by Margaret Noble, Irish by birth and British by citizenship but Indian by adoption and choice. She came to India as a disciple of Svāmī Vivekānanda in 1898 and was initiated into the Rāmakrṣna Order as a brahmacāriṇī (a celibate spiritual seeker) with the name Niveditā, the Dedicated.[2] Margaret Noble became a devotee of the Goddess and a child of Mother India, but her western rationalistic heritage never left her. Her prolific writings reveal her need to clarify for herself her perception of the social and political trends in India. At the same time, her writings mirror with remarkable sensitivity the ideals and the actual dynamics, the high hopes and the frustrating facts of the national movement in which she became a participant. The diverse political views and methods of the national leaders, many of whom she knew closely, are reflected in her writings.

The national movement of that period, especially in Bengāl where Niveditā lived and worked, had its base largely, if not exclusively, in the middle class that had been educated in

English. This factor explains why Nivedita, a western woman, could enter into the movement as fully as she did. Her numerous newspaper and journal articles were written at a time when journalism was both a powerful vehicle of self-expression and a binding force among the middle class.

Nivedita's writings bear witness to a period when the symbol of Mother India, emerging from a powerful living tradition of goddess worship, began to dominate the political scene. Her writings and speeches on Goddess Kālī and on Mother India sometimes appear to be a strange mixture of unleashed emotionalism and of careful critical judgment. She is caught up in the tide of the national movement and her experience is hardly that of a detached observer. For this very reason, her writings become a commentary on how the symbol of the Mother "works" in a specific socio-political context. As a consequence, her writings have value for those who study the significance of this symbol. They portray how the symbol affected the dynamics of a specific historical situation and how, in turn, the symbol took on further meanings from the socio-political trends.

Miss Margaret Noble (Nivedita) and the Indian National Movement

Miss Noble was the daughter of a Wesleyan minister, well-educated but acquainted with poverty. At the age of twenty-one, she worked in the mining town of Wrexham. At that time she wrote a series of powerful articles in support of the miners and their families. That reflected her special concern for the women of the district. Moved by human suffering and influenced by rationalistic thought, her dedication to Christian faith was gradually shaken. Such was her frame of mind when she met Svāmī Vivekānanda. In London in 1895 she had already opened her own school. She also had moved in literary circles frequented by Bernard Shaw and T.H. Huxley, had participated in Ireland's Home Rule movement, and had become known as a feminist. It took two years of thoughtful consideration before Svāmī Vivekānanda accepted her decision to join the Rāmakṛṣṇa Order and to work for the education of Indian women.[3] Her time in India was not long — she died in 1911, barely forty-four years of age — but was packed with momentous events led by extraordinary persons. Niveditā dedicated herself to the spirit of the time. The age, which witnessed a rising national consciousness, entered a new phase under the leadership of Bāl Gangādhar Tilak and Aurobindo Ghose (henceforth referred to as Aurobindo), who formed the Extremist party of the Indian National Congress. This new movement was born of an alliance between religion and politics: Mother India, perceived as an incarnation of the Divine Mother, became its rallying force and chosen symbol. Its exponents knew that nationalism would remain a foreign concept confined to the English-educated middle class unless it could be assimilated into traditional patterns of thought. In India, traditional moulds of thought have tended to be imbued with religion. But it would be incorrect to say that the Extremists deliberately chose the symbol of Mother India solely as a political expedient to popularize the national movement. Given the historical circumstances, the idea of Mother India sprang forth from the powerful living tradition of the Motherhood of God.

Svāmī Vivekānanda influenced the Extremists' aspiration for spiritual nationalism through his interpretation of Hinduism as the forerunner of an evolving universal religion. His "practical Vedānta" became the basis for the union of religion and politics. As Bipin Chandra Pāl has said, the new national movement was based on "the philosophy of the Absolute, the philosophy of Brahman as applied to the interpretation of man's social and civic life."[4]

Svāmī Vivekānanda sometimes referred to the figure of Mother India in his speeches. On one occasion he said, "For the next fifty years this alone shall be our keynote this, our great Mother India. Let all other vain gods disappear for the time from our minds."[5] The figure of Mother India, however, did not dominate his speeches, though Mother Kālī remained the focus of his personal devotion.[6] To avoid sectarian differences, he based his call to strength and "manliness" on the idea of the Indwelling Absolute (*antaryāmin*), which is taught in the Upaniṣads and is affirmed by all Hindus, rather than on the idea of Consciousness-energy (*śakti*), which is a special teaching of the Tantras.[7] (By contrast, Aurobindo's speeches focus on the idea of universal Consciousness-energy incarnate in Mother India.)

Once in India, Niveditā had to come to terms with "Vivekānanda, the Patriot," and "Vivekānanda, the son of Kālī." After many clashes of will with her guru, and after studying the situation in India, she retracted her stance that British rule was unquestionably good for India.[8] At the same time, she set herself to learn about Kālī like one learning a new language.[9] In this endeavour, Niveditā was deeply influenced by Śāradā Devī, disciple and wife of Śrī Rāmakṛṣṇa, spiritual mother of the Rāmakṛṣṇa Order and devotee of Kālī. Śāradā Devī opened her heart and home to Svāmī Vivekānanda's western disciples, laying aside the rules of Hindu orthodoxy.[10]

In 1899 Niveditā gave two public lectures on Kālī worship. Those present at the first lecture witnessed the strange spectacle of a western woman defending Kālī worship against westernized Bengālī critics of the Goddess. These critics were mainly members of the Brahmo Samāj who rejected image worship and recalled the social evils perpetrated by marginal groups among Kālī's devotees. Devotees and critics in the huge audience nearly rioted, and Niveditā had to restore calm. She was invited to give the second lecture at the foremost centre of goddess worship in Bengāl, the Kālīghāṭ temple.[11]

Niveditā's *Kālī the Mother*, published in 1900,[12] was written in the United States, where Svāmī Vivekānanda and she were trying to raise funds for the Rāmakṛṣṇa Mission. This book can be described as a testimony of personal devotion, except for one piece, "The Voice of the Mother," which stands apart in vocabulary and tone, thereby revealing Nivedita's growing political awareness. Here the sword, as a means of self-sacrifice, is presented as the very incarnation of the Goddess. Moreover, the Goddess is hailed as the "Mother of Nations." It has been pointed out that Nivedita's *Kālī the Mother* "deviated from the Hindu Āgamas and Nigamas in that it made the sword the incarnation of the Mother."[13] This work of Nivedita was generally well received, and it made a special mark on the younger generation of Indian nationalists. Aurobindo, for one, said that he was "very much enamoured" of *Kālī the Mother*.[14]

After the publication of *Kālī the Mother*, Svāmī Vivekānanda returned to India, but Nivedita went to her home in England, where she stayed until January 1902. Here she faced a dilemma. Up to that point she had adhered to Svāmī Vivekānanda's view that political development in India must follow from social reform, mass education and, above all, from massive religious awakening. While in England she came to accept the Extremist position that the political independence of India (*svarāj*) was the primary and immediate goal, and that national reconstruction could be viable only on the basis of political independence.[15]

After the death of Svāmī Vivekānanda in July 1902, Nivedita's association with the Rāmakṛṣna Order was formally ended by mutual consent, in order to give her full freedom for her political work.[16] Her school in Calcutta was left in the care of Sister Christine, another disciple of Svāmī Vivekānanda. Toward the end of that same year, Aurobindo met Nivedita for the first time. It is startling to read his statement that she was already a member of the secret revolutionary movement in Bengāl.[17] Aurobindo later appointed her as a member of a controlling committee of five, whose work it was to co-ordinate the revolutionary groups. This committee was unsuccessful in its task and soon ceased to exist. According to Aurobindo, there were "tens of thousands" in the revolutionary movement. They recognized each other as devotees of Śakti and were committed to the karmayoga (path of action) of the *Gītā*.

Passive resistance and svadeśi (the vow to use only goods made in India) were the methods put forward by the Extremist leaders to achieve the political freedom of India. While endorsing these methods, some among them, like Aurobindo, came to believe that an armed revolt might also one day be necessary.[18] The young revolutionaries were mainly of the educated middle class. Unemployment was a serious problem in Bengāl.[19] Bengālī youth were often accused of a lack of strength and integrity.[20] The most clear-sighted among the young revolutionaries knew that their sporadic acts of violence could not achieve political independence. Yet they hoped that by giving their lives for Mother India, they not only would clear themselves of the charge of cowardice, but also awaken their people and restore to them a measure of self-respect. An expression of such hope is found in a statement made by Madan Lāl Dangra before his execution in 1909:

> Poor in wealth and intellect a son like myself has nothing else to offer to the mother, but his own blood and so I have sacrificed the same on her altar. The only lesson required in India at present is to learn how to die and the only way to teach it is by dying ourselves ...[21]

It is difficult to gauge Niveditā's motives for supporting the revolutionaries and the extent of her involvement with them. One of her biographers, Lizelle Reymond, has claimed that she abetted their bomb-making experiments, and that she had to enter India in disguise after a trip abroad in 1911 to avoid the police. Barbara Foxe, another biographer, has denied all this.[22]

During the partition of Bengāl in 1905, Niveditā threw herself into the svadeśi movement. Svadeśi became a religious movement, with Mother India as its focus. Vows were made at the Kālīghāṭ temple to use only goods made in India.[23] Bankim Chandra Chatterjee's hymn to Mother India, *Bande Mātaram*, was sung in processions.[24] The myth of Durgā slaying the Buffalo Demon, Mahiṣāsura, was retold as the slaying of the demon of Manchester.[25]

In spite of her involvement with the revolutionaries, Niveditā maintained loyal friendships with Gokhale, the leader of the Moderates, with Romesh Dutt, who persuaded her to write *The Web of Indian Life*, and with Rabīndranāth Tagore. (The hero of Tagore's novel, *Gora*, like Niveditā, is also of Irish parentage, and Gora, like Niveditā, faces the dilemmas of those who cling to Hindu orthodoxy in the name of nationalism.)[26]

Niveditā's activities and associations were many-sided. She stood by Jagadīsh Chandra Bose at every step of his scientific work, and he and his wife cared for her in her last illness. She organized relief work when flood and famine hit East Bengāl in 1906. Always interested in art and archaeology, she supported the work of A.K. Coomaraswāmy and E.B. Havell. In a series of articles she made the public aware of the attempts of Abanīndranāth Tagore and Nandalāl Bose to evolve modern Indian styles of art.[27] She had a powerful influence on the patriot-poet Subramaṇia Bhārati.[28]

The turn of the century was a complex and volatile period in India, and the contradictory voices of the national leaders indicate their problems in interpreting the socio-political situation. Niveditā, bewildered often by what she saw, aspired to understand. If she succeeded to a large measure, it was because she gave her whole heart to India. As Rabīndranāth Tagore has said, she was in touch with the vital truths of Indian life:

> The life which Sister Nivedita gave for us was a
> very great life. There was no defrauding of us on
> her part, that is, she gave herself up fully for the
> service of India; she did not keep anything back

for her own use.... She was in fact a Mother of
People....[29]

The Hindu "Mother Church" and Indian Nationalism

The fundamental problem for Indian nationalism, as
Niveditā sees it, is the very concept of an Indian nation. She
maintains that India is one, and that all the diverse communities
of the subcontinent could be knit together by arousing, first, the
sense of a common homeland and, second, the feeling of a shared
historical evolution.[30] She argues, further, that the two great
empires in India, built by Aśoka and Akbar, were unified by
democratizing forces which were furnished, in the first case, by
the Buddhist ideal of compassion for all beings and, in the second,
by the Islamic affirmation of the brotherhood of man.[31]
    Her analysis remains superficial, however, for she
obscures the actual dynamics of the social situation in the
historical periods that she is discussing. Nevertheless, in spite of
the flaws in her analysis, the main thrust of her argument is clear.
She maintains that national consciousness cannot develop in India
unless the exclusivism of the Brāhmin tradition within Hinduism
is checked by the counterpoise of unifying and democratizing
forces.[32] Furthermore, she holds that external influences are
necessary to induce the development of democratizing forces
within the Hindu tradition. This is a hard admission for her, since
she is committed to defending Hindu values, including the caste
system. She concludes that the democratic values developed by
the reform movements of the nineteenth century through contacts
with the West could provide the basis for the unification of the
subcontinent as one nation.[33]
    Such is her commitment to Hinduism that she perceives
Indian nationality as a manifestation of the "Eternal Faith"
(sanātana dharma) of the Hindu "Mother Church." She points
out that Svāmī Vivekānanda gave a broad definition of the Hindu

tradition, including in its radius Buddhism, Jainism, Sikhism and all the religious sects originating under its influence.[34] She attaches the designation "Mother Church" to the Hindu tradition conceived in this broad, inclusive manner. Nivedita believes that, age by age, the Mother Church expresses herself differently, and that patriotism is the newest expression of a religion that steadfastly adores the One, though in diverse ways.[35]

Nivedita's conception of the Hindu Mother Church is simplistic. She does not perceive that Buddhism, Jainism and Sikhism would not want to be absorbed into Svāmī Vivekānanda's Neo-Vedānta. She is poignantly aware of the rifts between Hindus and Muslims,[36] but she does not face the fact that the idea of Hinduism as an all-assimilating Universal Religion — and, especially, her concept of the Hindu Mother Church as the matrix from which Indian nationalism evolves — would be viewed as a threat by Muslims. Her concept of the Hindu Mother Church illustrates how, within a concrete socio-political situation, the symbol of Motherhood could be used to represent and to foster that type of assimilation which allows growth only within the orbits of its controlling influence. Moreover, she says that the Hindu Mother Church must become "aggressive;"[37]

> The Eternal Faith must become active and pros-
> elytizing, capable of sending out special missions,
> of making converts, of taking back into her fold
> those of her children who have been perverted
> from her, and of the conscious and deliberate
> assimilation of new elements.[38]

She attributes these views to Svāmī Vivekānanda, but the term "aggressive Hinduism" does not appear in his public speeches, and the proselytizing spirit she envisages could be more correctly attributed to the Ārya Samāj than to the Rāmakṛṣṇa Mission.

More in line with Svāmī Vivekānanda's methods is her idea of reinterpreting the traditional ethical values of Hindu

Dharma to meet the needs of the modern age. She reaffirms his position that patriotic ideals will have no hold on the hearts of Hindus, unless they are perceived as genuine outgrowths of Dharma rather than as "foreign" notions precariously grafted on the minds of the middle class. She sets herself the task of interpreting the ideals of traditional Dharma in such a way that they may become the supports of national consciousness. Her aim is neither a mere "revival" of the tradition nor a "reform" that rejects the past, but a "recreating of the Dharma."[39] She "rereads" Dharma as sincerity, the integrity at the heart of things, "the substance, the self-ness, of things and of men."[40] She maintains that this integrity must be expressed as "National Righteousness,"[41] by which she means utter, unequivocal sincerity in service to the nation (jana-deśa-dharma).[42] According to her, "svadeśi tapasya" is the form that Dharma as National Righteousness must take to meet the need of the hour.[43] The Mother Church, she says, demands that the svadeśi vows taken at Kālīghāt be kept.

Niveditā is obviously following the trend set by Bankim, Svāmī Vivekānanda and Tilak in understanding karmayoga as the core of the Bhagavadgītā. Like them, she emphasizes integrity in daily work and national service, values relevant to the middle class of that period. In the fervour of national consciousness, she fails to see that when Dharma, traditionally interpreted as all-pervading cosmic law, is reduced to national dimensions, its meaning becomes drastically limited. Furthermore she re-reads the Gītā's message to signify that the avatāra (incarnation) comes from age to age "for the firm establishment of national righteousness."[44] Here she loses sight of the traditional belief in the cosmic outreach of the avatāra's task.

Mother India and the Mother Goddess

> He whom once we worshipped as Gopala, comes
> to us now in the guise of the Mother. He on
> Whose feet, as Narayana, we threw flowers, calls
> on us to offer lives and deaths instead.[45]

From a psychological perspective, it can be shown that
Nivedita's portrait of Mother India is drawn from her idealization
of Indian motherhood. In her defence of Indian women against
western critics of the *zenāna* system (separate living quarters for
women), Nivedita emphasizes that family life in India is centred
on the bond between a mother and her sons. In this bond, the
mother is both the protector and the protected: she is the protector
of her son, for she is spiritually strong, yet she needs to be
protected in other ways and, for her sake, he must grow to
manhood.[46]

Nivedita focuses on a tradition that Mother India is a
manifestation of Umā-Pārvatī. This Goddess is celebrated as
both mother and daughter. In her form as Durgā, she comes into
every home year by year during the Durgā festival, like a
daughter returning to her father's home. She is to be loved and
protected for she is the daughter, the "little mother."[47] Nivedita
transfers this twofold evocation of the Goddess as Protector
Mother and Protected Daughter to Mother India. For this reason,
she lavishes praise on Abanīndranāth Tagore's painting of
Mother India, where the Mother is portrayed as the ever-young
Goddess, Dawn.[48] She is the protector, offering with her four
hands gifts of faith (*dīkṣā*), learning (*śikṣā*), food (*anna*) and
clothing (*vastra*); she is to be protected, for she is tender and
vulnerable.

In *Kālī the Mother* the imagery changes: the Mother holds
in her hand not nourishing gifts but the sword of sacrifice.
Mother India is not mentioned in *Kālī the Mother*; but Kālī is
called "The Mother of Nations," and "The Voice of the

Mother"[49] is the call to service and self-sacrifice. "The Voice of the Mother" opens with the idea that the universe is the play of Kālī, her līlā. Her toy is the world-shattering thunderbolt. The Mother exchanges a secret sign with those who surrender their lives joyously to join her play: "Deep in the hearts of Mine own flashes the sacrificial knife of Kali. Worshippers of the Mother are they from their birth in Her incarnation of the sword."[50] Elsewhere Niveditā says that the devotees of the Mother are marked by "unflinching gaiety," for they are no longer moved by egoistic emotions of joy and sorrow: "The worship of the Mother is in truth the Vedanta of the hero. She is the whole, the Primal Force, the Infinite Power, the Adi-Shakti. To become one-d with that Power is to reach Samadhi."[51]

    Niveditā refers to a tradition that Ṛṣi Dadhīca gave his bones to make the thunderbolt.[52] Thus, for her, the thunderbolt (*vajra*) has a "secret meaning:" it signifies self-sacrifice.[53] Niveditā designed a national flag with a yellow vajra on a red background.[54] Those who sacrifice their lives to the Goddess become so many vajras held in her hands. Niveditā's interpretation of the "multiplying power"[55] of the vajra calls to mind the following lines from the *Bande Mātaram*:

> Terrible with the clamorous shout of
> seventy million throats,
> And the sharpness of swords raised in
> twice seventy million hands,
> Who sayeth to thee, Mother, that thou
> art weak?[56]

Niveditā's idea that the Mother herself becomes the "naked Sword of Purity," and that every self-sacrificing person is a vajra or sword in her hands, must have moved the revolutionaries. Aurobindo sings to Durgā, "We shall become thy instruments, thy sword slaying all evil."[57]

From the perspective of Nivedita's own life, "The Voice of the Mother" is puzzling on two counts. It was first published as early as 1898, but she did not enter the political scene until 1902. Moreover, she says that every word of it was garnered from Svāmī Vivekānanda.[58] In his speeches and writings, however, he did not endorse the use of violence in the nationalist movement. The most plausible explanation is that Nivedita did not write "The Voice of the Mother" to support the cause of the revolutionaries, although she later moved in that direction. In "The Voice of the Mother," Kālī speaks,

> Religion, called by whatever name, has been ever the love of death. But today the flame of renunciation shall be lighted in My lands and consume men with a passion beyond control of thought. Then shall My people thirst for self-sacrifice as others for enjoyment.... For this age is great in time, and I, even I, Kali, am the Mother of the nations.[59]

Again, in "The Call to Nationality," written when her ideas on Indian nationalism were more crystallized, Nivedita salutes the Goddess as the Mother of the nation, "Today She cries for the offering of Nationality.... Today She would that we play before Her with the sword."[60]

In the context of Nivedita's religious thought, the idea of Kālī as the Mother of Nations poses the following problem. The Hindu idea of Divine līlā or "play" is different from the idea of Divine will acting through the events of human history to accomplish Divine purposes. By hailing Kālī as the Mother of Nations, is Nivedita superimposing on the Hindu idea of līlā the Biblical notion of God acting through the critical moments of history to fulfil his purposes? Some of the speeches and writings of the Indian nationalists of Nivedita's time could be interpreted to mean that they believed that God's will was being served through their actions. For example, in a speech given after his release from jail, Aurobindo says that he heard the voice of God declaring, "It is the Shakti that has gone forth and entered into the people. Since long ago I have been preparing this uprising and now the time has come and it is I who will lead it to its fulfilment."[61] In his later writings Aurobindo clearly enunciates his view that the Goddess, in her immanent aspect, becomes the Divine Will guiding both the history of nations and the evolution of the universe towards a total spiritual transformation.

In Nivedita's works, one senses an unresolved tension between the idea of the Goddess as inexplicable māyā and the idea of the Goddess as purposeful Divine Will. In her lecture, "Kālī and Her Worship," she says, "Maya is false, Kali is its symbol. If Kali were painted as the ideal Hindu woman, she would have been real. To convey her unreality — as she shows herself, she is painted as the ideal *non*-woman." On the one hand, she interprets Kālī's dance on Śiva's body as a representation of the false and mirage-like quality of the universe. In her writings on nationalism, on the other hand, Kālī, playing with her naked sword, is the Mother of Nations, the guiding Divine Will in history, and Mother India is her incarnation.

The religious tradition of the Mother Goddess cut across regional, sectarian and caste boundaries; the influence of the political symbol of Mother India, however, remained largely confined to Bengāl, Mahārāshtra and Punjāb. The flow of historical events bears witness to the way the symbol of Mother India poured vitality into the national movement. Nevertheless, Aurobindo and the other leaders of the Extremist party did not succeed in creating a popular movement solely through the symbol of Mother India for the influence of this symbol only rarely went beyond the boundaries of the middle class. As a national symbol, Mother India had relevance for the middle class because it was convinced that its future destiny depended on fighting for a larger share in the political administration of India. In Bengāl the symbol became linked with the worship of Kālī, the

Mother in her form of Terror, because the educated youth of the Bengālī middle class came to realize that the prevailing socio-political situation demanded costly sacrifices from them. Without such sacrifices there was no hope of fulfilling their aspirations.

The rituals and symbols of traditional goddess worship are genuinely linked with the daily round of activities, the fears and hopes, of peasants and factory workers. The symbol of Mother India, however, failed to connect at the popular level and remained irrelevant to the people at large. Furthermore, by linking nationalism specifically with the renascent movements in modern Hinduism, the political symbol of Mother India not only failed as a vehicle of unification among the religious communities of the subcontinent but also undergirded the divisive trends in the national movement. Finally, the symbol of Mother India lost its momentum with the failure of the Extremist party. Caught in the swiftly moving political flow, Nived" tried to see the total picture and to interpret the course of these cross- currents both for herself, and for her friends, in the national movement.

The Evolution of India and the Divine Mother

Bankim Chandra Chatterjee's semi-historical Bengālī novel, *Ānandamaṭh*,[62] published in 1882, attained immediate and immense popularity largely because of the hymn to Mother India, *Bande Mātaram*, which appears in it. Nivedā's work, *Kālī the Mother*, published in 1900, consists of essays of devotion to the Goddess for the purpose of justifying Kālī worship to western readers and the educated middle class in India. Aurobindo's work, *Bhavānī Mandir*,[63] a tract for the secret revolutionary movement, was privately circulated during the partition of Bengāl (1905). Despite differences, these three works have a common theme: in all of them the historical evolution of India is linked with the Divine Mother who is perceived as the original Consciousness-force (*ādi-śakti*). The Goddess is celebrated as the one who protects and grants strength but also demands self-sacrifice.

Bankim's novel is based on the sannyāsin rebellions that followed the Bengāl famine of 1768-1770. In the novel, a secret order of sannyāsins who are fighting for the liberation of the motherland from Muslim rule gather in a hidden temple where they worship Mother India in her three aspects.[64] The magnificent Jagaddhātrī is "the Mother as she *was*;" Kālī, gaunt, naked and wretched, trampling on her own Good,[65] is "the Mother as she has *now* become;" Durgā, radiant and powerful, is "the Mother as she *would be*." *Bande Mātaram* is their hymn of adoration to this goddess for whom they give their lives. Bipin Chandra Pāl has elucidated the powerful impact of this novel. The traditional goddesses who had lost their hold on the educated middle class were "reinstalled with a new historic and nationalistic interpretation."[66] They came to be perceived as "symbolic of the different stages of national evolution,"[67] and as different manifestations of the Mother who is "the spirit of India."

It is not impossible that Svāmī Vivekānanda was influenced by Bankim's idea of a patriotic order of sannyāsins. Unlike Bankim, he rejected the idea of sannyāsins engaging in warfare or engineering political movements. However, Bankim's own preface to the first edition of this novel is often forgotten. Here he declared, "Revolutions are very generally processes of self-torture and rebels are suicides. The English have saved Bengāl from anarchy."[68] In the light of this preface, we can only speculate whether, in fact, Bankim would have endorsed the violent side of the revolutionary movement in Bengāl.

Svāmī Vivekānanda convinced the Rāmakṛṣṇa Order that, in the modern age, the needs of Indian society demanded a working order of sannyāsins engaged in mass education and social reconstruction.[69] It was at the temple of the Goddess Kanyā Kumārī that the idea of a working order of sannyāsins had taken shape in his mind.[70] Mother India as Virgin Daughter was to be cared for and protected. Svāmī Vivekānanda also asked his

countrymen to build temples, non-sectarian in character and
marked only by the symbol *Om*, which would become centres to
serve the people.[71] These centres, of course, were to be out in
the open and not hidden like the secret temple of *Ānandamath*.

Aurobindo, on the contrary, did conceive of gathering a
secret order of sannyāsins and brahmacārins who, like the
sannyāsins of *Ānandamath*, would train themselves for armed
revolt. His brother Barīndra tried unsuccessfully to find a remote
place for a temple to the Goddess Bhavānī that would serve as a
centre for the revolutionaries.[72] In *Bhavānī Mandir* Aurobindo
maintains that Rāmakrṣṇa had come into the world to initiate the
rebirth of India, and that Svāmī Vivekānanda had preached the
way of strength.[73] He believed that they had paved the way for
the revolutionary movement.

Though Svāmī Vivekānanda did not countenance secret
movements or the use of violence, his call for strength was like
dynamite to the young revolutionaries. For example, he exhorts,

> Say brother: "the soil of India is my highest
> good," and repeat and pray day and night, "O
> Thou Lord of Gauri, O Thou Mother of the Uni-
> verse, vouchsafe manliness unto me! O Thou
> Mother of Strength, take away my weakness and
> make me a Man!"[74]

Niveditā and Aurobindo came to believe that this call to strength
could only be answered through a revolutionary movement. It has
been said that Svāmī Vivekānanda's works "were found in every
house that the Bengāl Police searched during the Swadeshi
era."[75]

Conclusion

The idea of Mother India, the Mother Goddess, and Militancy, raises several significant questions in the context of modern Hinduism. From the point of view of Hindu spirituality, a critic may well question the adequacy of the symbol. Niveditā points out that according to the Hindu tradition, a genuine symbol is one which constantly points beyond every meaning attributed to it: "of all the peoples on earth, it might be claimed that Hindus are apparently the most, and at heart the least, idolatrous. For the application of their symbols is many-centred, like fire in opals."[76] Traditionally, a genuine symbol impels the devotee to enter ever-new dimensions of religious experience until union with the Ultimate Being is realized. It can be argued that the modern symbol of Mother India narrows the devotee's perception rather than compelling it to expand toward the vision of Kālī as the infinite Mother of infinite space and time. If Kālī is the symbol of primordial power, Kālī must be energizing the enemies of India as well as nationalists fighting her cause. Perhaps it was this realization that came to Svāmī Vivekānanda at Kṣirbhāvanī. He said that he heard the Mother asking him: "What if unbelievers should enter My temple and defile My image? What is that to you? Do you protect Me, or do I protect you?" Then he felt the narrowing boundaries of his patriotism fall away from him: "now it is only 'Mother, Mother! I have been very wrong...'"[77]

The symbol of Mother India can narrow the perception of the devotee precisely because it has the inherent inadequacy of being too concrete in its immediate denotation. In traditional Hindu worship, Durgā, Kālī and Jagaddhatrī point beyond the sacred places with which their names may be associated, because their actions are conceived as taking place in the vastness of mythic time and space. Traditional Hinduism does not bind its symbols of infinite Divine presence to concrete historical events that can be dated. The symbol of Mother India inevitably becomes connected with the concrete events of the nation's history and the patriotic aspirations of its people. As a consequence, there is the danger that the symbol might narrow the vision of the nationalist devotee to national boundaries. If this happens, the symbol would not impel the consciousness of the devotee towards an awareness of all-pervading Divine presence. It would not fulfil the function demanded of its spiritual symbols by the Hindu tradition. From the point of view of the spiritual aspirations towards infinity expressed in the Hindu tradition, then, this danger of bondage to national history is the source of the inadequacy of the symbol of Mother India.

From the point of view of the nation's social and economic development, it can be argued that the symbol of Mother India is inadequate because it tends to focus the mind on an idealized picture of India, rather than on the concrete needs of society. The Extremists in the Indian National Congress used the symbol of Mother India to buttress their argument that the political independence of India must first be achieved in order that efforts towards social reform and economic development might be fruitful. It is a sad paradox that the revolutionary youth inspired by the symbol of the sword were willing to die for the liberation of Mother India, but seldom were able to live and labour in the field of social reconstruction for the people of India. Niveditā, too, forgot the concrete and immediate needs of her school in Calcutta in her zeal for the revolutionary movement. For Svāmī Vivekānanda, Mother India signified the people of India: but he had walked through the length and breadth of India as a pilgrim.

Psychological and sociological studies have shown that the symbol of the Mother represents a primordial, all-inclusive energy that both creates and reabsorbs all beings into itself. The symbol, therefore, signifies a power that ultimately no being can resist or oppose. As a symbol of all-inclusiveness, the figure of Mother India became the dynamic force behind two distinct trends in the national movement. On the one hand, the symbol was interpreted in such a way as to signify a creative unity including and accepting differences. Niveditā argued that the different communities of the subcontinent could enrich each other as children of one Mother. On the other hand, Niveditā and some Hindu nationalists interpreted the all-inclusiveness of the Mother as a type of assimilation that reabsorbs everything into its sovereign influence. The symbol intensified their tendency to think in terms of assimilating all the communities of the subcontinent into a nation which they conceived to be Hindu in its culture and ideals. This tendency could not but alienate the Muslims and all others who opposed such assimilation.

In the final analysis, it was the idea of the Goddess as primordial energy that most profoundly influenced Niveditā, Aurobindo and other leaders of the Extremist party. According to the Hindu tradition, the Mother as ultimate Consciousness-energy (*cit-śakti*) is both transcendent and immanent. In her essential nature, wisdom and power are unified. As ultimate Consciousness, she transcends human distinctions of good and evil and manifests herself as the wisdom that overcomes all ignorance. As ultimate energy she becomes the matrix of evolution and manifests herself as the source of all motivation, both good and evil.

In the context of the national movement in which Niveditā participated, the symbol of the Mother, interpreted as immanent all-conquering energy, endowed the middle class with a much needed sense of self-respect. The symbol empowered it to assume leadership in a period when its economic resources were curtailed and its political aspirations constantly frustrated. However, given the contingencies of the political context, the leaders found it difficult to hold together the values of transcendent wisdom and immanent power. They focused on one side of the symbol — on the idea of the Goddess as all-pervading power — rather than on the "bi-unity" of wisdom and power, which is the central meaning of the symbol of the Mother within the Hindu tradition. The symbol then displayed its dark side. It influenced some of the revolutionaries to deploy power indiscriminately, and sometimes violently, as a means to an end that they perceived to be good.

Perhaps it is because Motherhood as a symbol connotes primordial, undifferentiated energy that Mahātma Gandhi chose not to make Mother India the dominant symbol of the movement that he led. He chose satyam (truth) rather than śakti (power) to be the nation's ideal. Niveditā met Mahātma Gāndhi once, in 1902.[78] They had little to say to each other at that time, and parted company.

Notes

1. Sister Nivedita, *The Complete Works of Sister Nivedita*, ed. Pravrajika Atmaprana, 2nd ed. (Calcutta: Sister Nivedita Girls' High School, 1972), II:267 (hereafter referred to as CWN).

2. This sketch of Sister Niveditā's life is based on the following two biographies: Lizelle Reymond, *The Dedicated* (Madras: Samata Books, 1985); Barabara Foxe, *Long Journey Home* (London: Rider and Company, 1975).

3. In July 1897, Svāmī Vivekānanda wrote to Margaret Noble: "Let me tell you frankly that I am now convinced that you have a great future in the work for India. What was wanted was not a man, but a woman; a real lioness, to work for the Indians, women especially."

   "India cannot yet produce great women, she must borrow them from other nations" (CWN, I:vii).

4. Cited in K.C. Chaudhry, *Role of Religion in Indian Politics (1900-1925)* (Delhi: Sundeep Prakashan, 1978), 45.

5. Swāmī Vivekānanda, *The Complete Works of Swami Vivekananda*, 8th ed. (Calcutta: Advaita Ashrama, 1964-72), III:300 (Hereafter referred to as CWV).

6. In a letter to Mary Hale, Vivekānanda writes, "The Upani-
    shads teach us all there is of Religion. Kali worship is my
    special *fad*; you never heard me preach it, or read of my
    preaching it in India" (CWV, VIII:522-523).

7. CWV, III:130-131, 160, 191, 225, 237, 244, 284, 318.

    It is interesting to compare Nivedita's approach to goddess
    worship with that of Sir John Woodroffe, who came to India
    in 1890. One of his aims was to make educated Indians
    aware of their Tantra heritage. For example, to establish
    that the idea of universal Consciousness-energy was compat-
    ible with modern knowledge, he referred to Jagadīsh
    Chandra Bose's research on consciousness in plants. The
    primary thrust of his work, however, was based on the
    scholarly interpretation of texts. Nivedita, too, displayed a
    scholarly interest in the origins of goddess worship and its
    regional differences, but, unlike Woodroffe, she also
    conveyed the ardour of a devotee. For a discussion of Sir
    John Woodroffe's role in the development of Tantricism in
    modern Bengal, see N.N. Bhattacharyya, "Neo-Tantric
    Movements in the Nineteenth and Twentieth Centuries" in
    S.P. Sen, ed., *Social and Religious Reform Movements in
    the Nineteenth and Twentieth Centuries* (Calcutta: Institute
    of Historical Studies, 1979).

8. Foxe, 33, 41-44, 48-50.

9. *The Master as I Saw Him*, in CWN, I:117.

10. CWN I:103-111.

11. Foxe, 80-85.

12. *Kali the Mother* is included in CWN, Vol. I.

13. Keshab Choudhri, "Religion as the Language of Political Radicalism," in *Calcutta Journal of Political Studies*, I, No. 1 (Winter 1980).

14. Aurobindo Ghose, *Sri Aurobindo*, Sri Aurobindo Birth Centenary Library (Pondicherry: Sri Aurobindo Ashram Trust, 1972); Vol. 26, *Sri Aurobindo on Himself*, 58, 69. (This series is hereafter referred to as SABCL).

15. Foxe, 125-128. In a letter to a friend, Niveditā says that her life had come to include "many elements that Svāmi would probably not have put there." She continues, "And I belong to Hinduism more than ever I did, but I see the *political* need so clearly, too!" (128).

16. Foxe, 150.

17. SABCL, Vol. 26, *Sri Aurobindo on Himself*, 69.

18. Ambalal B. Purani, *The Life of Sri Aurobindo*, (Pondicherry: Sri Aurobindo Ashram, 1964), 96; Srinivasa Iyengar, *Sri Aurobindo: A Biography and A History*, 2 Vols. (Pondicherry: Sri Aurobindo International Centre of Education, 1972), I:109, 487-488.

19. Sukhbir Choudhary, *Growth of Nationalism in India*, 2 Vols. (New Delhi: Trimurti Publications, 1973), I:185-186.

20. See, for example, the convocation address at Calcutta University in 1905 by Lord Curzon. For excerpts from this address, and for a discussion of other disparaging accounts of Indians given by British officials in that period, see Choudhary, *Growth of Nationalism in India*, I:104, 124-136, 148, 382. The repeated call to "manliness" made by Niveditā and the Indian nationalists must be seen in this context. Niveditā wrote an article in the *Amrita Bazar*

Patrika, which included a quotation from Curzon's book, *Problems of the Far East* (London, 1894) to illustrate his own lack of honesty (Foxe, 173).

21. Cited in Chaudhry, 147.

22. Reymond, 280-287, 336-338, 345; Foxe, 169-170, 204.

23. Chaudhry, 74-75; Nemai Sadhan Bose, *The Indian Awakening and Bengal* (Calcutta: Firma K.L. Mukhopadhyay, 1969), 250-254.

24. For a description of the powerful influence of the *Bande Mātaram*, especially on Bengāli youth, see Iyengar, 366-367. Iyengar says, "The traditional religious worship of Mother Durga merged with the patriotic adoration of the country as the Mother, and so Durga and Bharati fused into Bhavani, 'holder of multitudinous strength — *bahubala dhāriṇī*'" (I:367).

25. Chaudhry, 72.

26. Reymond, 174-175.

27. CWN, Vol. III includes her articles on Indian Art.

28. Iyengar, I:369.

29. CWN, I:xi.

30. *Civic Ideal and Indian Nationality* in CWN, IV:264-270.

31. CWN, IV:308.

32. Niveditā writes, "Hinduism alone, in its completeness, can never create a nationality, for then it tends to be dominated by the *exclusivism* of the Brahmin caste ... It is only,

therefore, when there is within Hinduism itself, a counter-centre to the Brahmin, that Hinduism can suffice to create a nationality" (CWN IV:261-262).

33. For Niveditā, democracy in India signifies the awakening of the women and the masses. She writes, "For in looking to the growth of a sentiment of nationality as the solution of Indian problems, we are of course turning away from kings and priests, and appealing to Women and the People" (CWN, II:239).

34. CWN, I:7, 113, 161. Svāmī Vivekānanda, of course, does not use the term "Mother Church" except as an affectionate nickname for his friend, Mrs. Hale.

35. CWN, III:467.

36. CWN, IV:291; II:242.

37. *Aggressive Hinduism* in CWN, Vol. III.

38. CWN, I:161.

39. CWN, V:85.

40. CWN, III:418.

41. CWN, III:465.

42. CWN, V:170.

43. CWN, IV:279-281.

44. CWN, II:140.

45. CWN, III:467.

46. CWN, II:17, IV:252-253, 266.

47. CWN, II:23, 324.

48. CWN, III:57-60.

49. CWN, I:493-494.

50. CWN, I:493-494. Śivāji was a devotee of the Goddess Bhavānī, and it was a custom in the Marāthā army to call the sword by the name of Bhavānī (Phillip Spratt, *Hindu Culture and Personality* [Bombay: Manaktalas, 1967], 240, 349. It is possible that Niveditā was aware of this Marāthā tradition.

51. CWN, III:420.

52. J.A.B. van Buitenen, trans., *Mahābhārata* (The University of Chicago Press, 1980), I:281.

53. CWN, V:168.

54. CWN, V:166-167.

55. Niveditā refers to the traditional design where one vajra is laid across another, and it is interpreted as a symbol of multiplication.

56. SABCL, Vol. 8, *Translation from Sanskrit and other Languages*, 313.

57. Iyengar, I:517.

58. CWN, I:116.

59. CWN, I:494.

60. CWN, IV:295.

61. Purani, 120.

62. Nares Chandra Sen-gupta, trans., *The Abbey of Bliss* (Calcutta: Padmini Mohan Neogi). The first thirteen chapters of *Ānandamath* were translated by Aurobindo and serialized in the *Karmayogin* in 1909. This translation is included in SABCL, Vol. 8.

63. The complete text of *Bhavānī Mandir* appears in Purani, 75-86.

64. Sen-gupta, 38-42.

65. Sen-gupta 41. The translator adds, in a footnote, "The form of Siva under Kali's feet the author takes to be an allegorical representation of 'Good,' for Siva means 'good.'" Aurobindo translates, "Her own God she tramples under her feet."

66. Cited in Kalinkar Datta, *Renaissance, Nationalism and Social Change in Modern India* (Calcutta: Bookland Private Ltd. 1965), 9.

67. Cited Chaudhry, 46.

68. Sen-gupta, xii.

69. See Svāmī Vivekānanda's letters to the monks of the Rāmakṛṣṇa order (CWV, VI:254-255, 266, 288, 294.

70. Swami Nikhilananda, *Vivekananda: A Biography* (Calcutta: Advaita Ashrama, 1964), 99-100; CWV, VI:254.

71. CWN, III:302-303.

72. Iyengar, I:315.

73. Purani, 80.

74. CWV, IV:480.

75. Nemai Sadhan Bose, *The Indian Awakening and Bengal* (Calcutta: Firma K.L. Mukhopadhyay, 1960), 167.

76. CWN, I:468.

77. Nikhilananda, 276.

78. Foxe, 134-135.

FEMALE WARRIORS, MAGIC AND THE SUPERNATURAL IN TRADITIONAL CHINESE NOVELS

Fan Pen Chen

Precursors of the female generals in Peking Operas as well as of the swordswomen of the modern *kung fu* (*wuxia*) novels and films,[1] women warriors had existed in the military romance (*yanyi*) genre of Chinese novels since the Ming (1368-1644). The military romance proliferated from the Ming to the Qing (1644-1911). It was eventually transformed into and displaced in popularity by the *kung fu* genre of novels. Considerably shorter than the voluminous *kung fu* novel, however, the military romance is generally around 80 to 100 chapters each. While the *kung fu* novel shares with the military romance the dependence of its protagonists on tutelage by celestials and mastery of magic, the former features mainly swordmen and women seeking personal vendettas. It is in the military romance that one finds warriors and generals, many of whom being female, lead entire armies against enemy troops.

Aside from presenting characteristics of women warriors, this study will analyze their significance in terms of the *yin-yang* paradigm. As embodiments of the *yin*, the appeal of these fictional characters reflects the fantasies and desires of their traditional Chinese readers. Their strength and power also manifest the importance of the *yin* for the protection of the *yang*.

Curiously, the two most famous historical women warriors are conspicuously insignificant in the military romance. Probably due to limitations forced upon their characterization because of their historicity, Hua Mulan (referred to as Fa Mu Lan in Maxine Hong's *The Women Warrior*) and Liang Hongyü are but second rate warriors in *Military Romance of Sui and Tang* (*Sui Tang yanyi*)[2] and *The Yuefei Saga* (*Jingzhong Yuezhuan; Shuo Yue quanzhuan*)[3] respectively. The female warriors Gu Dasao, Sun Erniang and Hu Sanniang in *Water Margin* (*Shuihu zhuan*), just as Lady Zhuyong in *Romance of the Three Kingdoms* (*Sankuo yanyi*) are similarly essentially second-rate fighters. They lack lustre when compared to the predominantly fictional heroines to be discussed, mainly due to the fact that they do not employ magic.

Female warriors must rely on supernatural powers and magical weapons to outshine their male counterparts. Almost all of the most powerful women warriors possess magical powers and weapons bestowed upon them by Daoist (Taoist) celestials. In fact, Ziya, the military advisor in *Investiture of the Gods* (*Fengshen yanyi*)[4] cautions his warriors against three types of opponents: Taoist priests, monks, and women, since these are the people who usually command magical arts.[5]

In *Investiture of the Gods*, Princess Longji is an immortal in exile while Deng Shanyü defeats many an enemy with supernatural five-colored stones. Mu Gueiying in *Warriors of the Yang Family* (*Yangjiajiang yanyi*)[6] possesses three throwing knives which strike with deadly precision. In *The Yuefei Saga*, Luanying wins by throwing two magical stone objects and Little Girl Xiyun (*Xiyun xiaomei*) uses two pellets called yin-yang pellets and a 'white dragon belt' which when thrown into the air turns into a dragon that wraps itself around the enemy. Diao Yue'o in *Three Tales from the Tang* (*Shuo Tang Sanzhuan*)[7] renders her foes unconscious by ringing a 'soul-capturing' bell.

In *Unofficial History of a Female Celestial* (*Nüxian waishi*, hereafter *Female Celestial*),[8] the Daoist celestial general Tang Saier, who is also reincarnated from the goddess of the moon, can predict the weather and 'shrink the earth' to shorten travel time for her army. Many of the female warriors serving her also perform magic. The swordswoman She Yinniang, for example, once transforms pieces of wood into an army of giant guards to protect their camp.[9]

The women warriors in *Three Tales from the Tang* are most conspicuously disciples of female celestials.[10] Xue Jinlian obtained supernatural powers through the tutelage of a 'celestial mother.' Dou Xiantong who excels in the use of a magic lasso is a disciple of the Saintly Mother of Yellow Flower. Chen Jinding is a disciple of the Wudang Celestial School, while Fan Lihua, the most powerful of them all, is a disciple of the Saintly Mother of Mount Li. Among other tricks, she is capable of moving mountains and oceans, and creating people and horses out of beans and grass.

Confronted with the extraordinary powers of such women warriors, the men of the opposite camp must rely on celestials to attempt to win. Most of these celestials are Daoist immortals, many of whom being animals that have attained the *dao*.[11] They parade themselves in human form, usually as priests or priestesses, or even as gods and goddesses, and revert back to their original forms only after suffering defeat. Beastly and evil by nature, these celestials include transformations of tortoises, crabs, cranes, various types of dragon, snakes, lions, tigers, bears, buffaloes, fish, horses, cocks, dogs and foxes.

In *Three Tales from the Tang*, a 'perverted dragon' who arrives as a Daoist priest to avenge the death of one of his human disciples, reveals his beastly nature through his culinary preference.

> The barbarian soldiers brought in wine and food but the Daoist priest was not satisfied. So he said, "My dear barbarians, my master at Longzhou was in the habit of eating live pigs and sheep. If you have any, do bring them over right away so that I can feast myself." When the barbarian soldiers heard him, they immediately brought him a pig

and a sheep. The Daoist priest was delighted. He carved open their hearts with a knife, sucked up the warm blood, and then sliced the meat and ate it. In no time at all, they were completely consumed.[12]

Powerful women warriors, on the other hand, are characteristically magnificently clad creatures of exceptional beauty. The following description of Fan Lihua in *Three Tales from the Tang* is a typical example.

> Wearing a crown of golden phoenix decorated with two pheasant feathers, her face resembled Xizi,[13] her appearance, that of Zhaojun.[14] Her beauty would put to shame the moon and all flowers; it even surpassed that of Chang O in the moon.[15] Clad in a golden armour of knotted chains, and covered with an embroidered dragon cloak, she wore a pair of tiny satin boots.[16] She rode a cloud-ascending horse and wielded a pair of knives.[17]

Armed with magical powers, women warriors would defeat their male counterparts with ease until they confront celestial opponents possessing similar powers. The fighting scene then turns into a celestial battle of the good against the evil. The following scene demonstrates a short combat of this type.

> The two fought a few rounds. And then Tianshen[18] feigned defeat and ran away, goading Madame Du to chase after him in pursuit. He then performed sorcery by chanting a magic formula. Suddenly heaven and earth darkened and a furious wind raged. From the sky, forty-nine black baneful demons descended, each brandishing a sharp

weapon. The Song soldiers were terrified. Angri-
ly, Madame Du exclaimed, "You might get away
with using such an evil trick on others, but how
dare you use it on me?" She thereupon began to
chant a secret magic formula obtained from the
True Celestial of Jinhua. In no time at all, peals of
thunder began to burst, the entire sky burned with
balls of fire which decimated all the demons and
barbarian warriors. And then heaven and earth
regained light.[19]

Most of the wars expand from normal fights into such
celestial battles of ever-ascending magnitude. Magical military
formations (*zhen*) are invariably designed by celestials supporting
the side of the evil — the side that will ultimately lose, be it a
barbarian state fighting against Chinese forces or a 'bad' Chinese
emperor destined to be displaced. Ingenious and deadly, these
formations require great skill and magical powers to 'break' and
destroy. They vary from the simple one created by Saintly
Mother of Golden Lights quoted below, to highly complicated
ones even more grotesque.

The Saintly Mother of Golden Lights said, "My
formation of the golden lights contains the essence
of the sun and the moon, and the energy of heaven
and earth. In it there are twenty-one magical
mirrors which are hung onto the tops of twenty-
one poles. The mirrors are enclosed in bags.
When a human being or a celestial enters the formation, the bags can be lifted off, peals of thunder
will then shake the mirrors causing them to rotate
and emanate light. As soon as the golden lights
strike the intruder, he will melt into a pool of
blood. Even those who can fly will have trouble
traversing this formation unscathed.[20]

In one of the mazes of a most elaborate formation created by none
other then Lü Dongbin, one of the Eight Daoist Immortals, a
foreign princess stands in the nude with a skull in her hand. She
is supposed to render the enemy unconscious by weeping out loud
when she encounters them. In another maze of this formation,
seven pregnant women are buried upside down to suck the
enemy's spirit.[21] The unorthodox and weird methods used in
the set-up of such formations[22] underscore the evil which the
heroines must combat. Hence, the most outstanding women
warriors must be able to analyze, name and annihilate such formations.

One of the most striking characteristics of many women
warriors is their barbaric origin. The majority of them are either
foreign princesses or daughters of bandit-chieftains. They speak
Chinese and seem no different from Chinese female warriors
except for their ready passion and forwardness in the pursuit of
love.

Young warriors usually meet their future mates initially
through combat. The Chinese female warrior, however, never
shows any interest in men. Unless her father intervenes and
arranges the marriage for her,[23] she has to be either tricked or
forced into compromising herself before she would agree to
marriage.[24] The barbarian female warrior, on the other hand,
tends to be the wooer rather than the wooed. She is neither
hindered by moral scruples nor ashamed in the pursuit of her
chosen mate.

Foreign princess warriors in these novels are ineluctably
attracted to Chinese warriors who are admired more for their
beauty than for their prowess.[25] When Little Girl Xiyun sees the
Chinese warrior Wu Lian, she thinks to herself,

> If he isn't a reincarnation of Pan An,[26] he must
> be a live Buddha from the western heaven. When
> have I ever seen anyone so handsome in our
> barbarian state? Why don't I capture the Southern

barbarian[27] alive and marry? I wouldn't have lived in vain then.[28]

The bandit princess Dou Xiantong in *Three Tales from the Tang* similarly attracted by Xue Dingshan's "face so white, it was as if he had used powder; lips so red, it was as if he had applied rouge."[29] Indeed, the military success achieved by many warriors seem dependent on their ability to attract foreign princesses.

Many accept the capitulation of these beauties wholeheartedly. After all, they not only get the girl and her military might, but also her army and possessions. One of the most convenient ways to defeat the enemy is to marry his daughter and get him on one's own side. Once Han Qilong and Niu Tong had compromised the warrior daughters of two commanders of strategic passes, therefore, they had also gained access to the passes. It is not surprising, then, that Liu Shi in *Warriors of the Yang Family* readily accepts the offers of marriage from the foreign princesses Huang Qiongnü[30] and Chong Yangnü.[31] And the two brothers Liu Ren and Liu Rui in *Three Tales from the Tang* are more than willing to comply with marriage proposals from their captors, two beautiful princesses. These princesses not only wed the handsome brothers but also capitulate to the Tang, the reigning dynasty.[32]

Some Chinese warriors, however, are most reluctant to submit to the advances of these passionate women. As powerless captives, they cling to Confucian principles to boost their manly pride. They denounce the immoral passion of the female warriors, only to swear false oaths in order to escape. Such warriors resent the change of roles in courtship and would rather marry an ugly or weaker woman than the beauties who desire them. But in stooping to expediency and betraying their own words, the men are shown less heroic than the women warriors who have decided to stake everything for love. The fate of such foreign princesses can be tragic, especially if they do not receive support from the men's families.

The story of Little Girl Xiyun is a case in point. Her infatuation for the handsome Wu Lian seals her fate. As her captive, Wu agrees to marriage on the condition that she kill her commander. She fulfills her part of the bargain by refusing to assist the superior in battle, but he continually stalls the consummation of the marriage until he manages to escape. Finding himself in the bedroom of the commander's daughter by chance, he rapes her and then promises to avenge her father's death. This promise is fulfilled the following day when Wu hacks Little Girl Xiyun into halves across her waist. He then crowns his success with marriage to the commander's daughter who now surrenders to the Song, the reigning Chinese dynasty.[33] Events characteristically work out to the benefit of the Chinese male warriors.

The desire of some military families to harness the power of valorous women warriors may prove to be girl's only chance. In *Warriors of the Yang Family*, Yang Zongbao feigns agreement to the marriage proposal from My Guiying, daughter of a local prince and leader or an army of bandits, in order to save his own life and obtain a desperately needed magical weapon from her. When she arrives at his camp, she is repudiated by his father until she proves her military prowess. Mu is then welcomed into the family as his daughter-in-law.[34]

Xue Dingshan, in *Three Tales from the Tang*, must be nominated the most sexy male warrior. Women, especially foreign female warriors are so irresistibly attracted to him that they would capture him only to surrender to him with the intention of marrying him. He ends up taking three martial wives, all superior to him in the battlefield. Even a barbarian queen lusts after him following a field encounter.[35]

Xue Dingshan's marriages reveal the importance of expediency when weighed against that of personal pride and preference. His first wife is the sister of a bandit-chieftain, who, upon capturing Dingshan, becomes so enamoured that she proposes marriage to him. He denounces her and rejects her until his parents intervene.[36] Dingshan's second wife is the daughter of a hunter and exceptionally ugly. Despite her appearance, however, and possibly because of her non-aggressive attitude after saving his life, he takes her as wife. His third romance is the most fascinating one, with probably the most famous female warrior in Chinese novels.

Infatuated with Dingshan and determined not to marry the ugly barbarian warrior chosen by her parents, Fan Lihua betrays her state, kills her father by accident and then her two brothers in self-defense. Armed with magic more powerful than that of any other warrior in the novel, she has the support of Dingshan's family, which repeatedly promises his agreement to consummate their marriage whenever Lihua's military skills become indispensable to their war efforts. Reluctant to submit to parental pressure and probably also suffering from an inferiority complex, he consistently breaks his promises and repudiates her. She eventually obtains the backing of the emperor who orders Dingshan to enlist her assistance. After humiliating him at length, she feigns death and finally earns the love of the repentent husband.

While the passion of the foreign female warrior[37] must have fascinated Chinese readers, her infatuation for Chinese warriors reflects male fantasy. The willing submission of such princesses means free women, power and wealth. That foreign princesses would invariably find the effeminate beauty of Chinese warriors irresistable, constitutes a Chinese fantasy. Finally, the fact that the success of a female warrior in her pursuit of love by a reluctant man is depedent on her possession of military skills needed by his family, bespeaks of the impossibility of such situations in real life.

Military romances are fictions. They tell us more about the fantasies and fascinations of their readers than about social realities. They reflect the operation of opposing cosmic forces of the time more than stark realities. In terms of the *yin-yang* paradigm, or the female-male complementary components of the cosmos, women warriors can be seen as forces of the *yin* that, in these novels, are necessary for the suppression of evil and protection of the *yang*.

While Confucianism, the dominant elite ideology, has been associated with the *yang*, Daoism has always been characterized as *yin*. The main classic of the Daoist philosophy, the *Daodejing* described the *dao* or the Way as being rooted in a 'mysterious female.'

> This spirit of the valley never dies.
> This is called the mysterious female.
> The gatway of the mysterious female
> Is called the root of heaven and earth.[38]

Associated with nature and darkness, the *yin* originally co-existed with the *yang* on an equal footing. The two forces complemented each other and must be present in equal amounts to preserve cosmic balance. But as China became increasingly patriarchal from the Zhou dynasty (1115-221 B.C.) on, the *yang* took on positive values while the *yin* suffered degradation and eventually came to be associated with evil.

When characterizing the dichotomy between the Chinese and their enemies, the Chinese represent the forces of the *yang*, while the barbarians represent that of the *yin*. In fact, all that is rational and orthodox is *yang*, while that which is irrational and unorthodox is considered *yin*.

Women warriors are basically creatures symbolizing forces of the *yin*. They possess one attribute associated with forces of the *yang* — namely, their military prowess. But aside from this one aspect they are creatures of the *yin*. They are female, predominantly barbarians, given to passion, use magic and are disciples of Daoist celestials. The fascination of Chinese readers for these female warriors, hence, reflects a longing for fulfillment of the libido — for the magical, the passionate, the barbaric. Indeed, these passionate female warriors of foreign origin seem to symbolize the dark energies of the subconscious to which the traditional Chinese reader must have felt drawn.

The enemies of the protagonist are necessarily evil. Often foreign armies, they depend on sorcery and the creation of magical military formations by wayward Daoist celestials. Chinese warriors do not stand a chance against such opponents without the aid of female warriors and their magic. Hence, the *yin* in the form of the woman warrior is needed to combat forces that are even more *yin*.

During Fan Lihua's most challenging campaign against a host of Daoist celestials, she is trapped within a most formidable military formation. The day of heavy fighting has induced her to go into labor and she finally falls from her horse in pain. The enemy general combating her immediately uses his treasured magical flying sword on her.

> A red light shot up from her, however, and turned the flying sword into ash. Greatly angered, Baotong [the enemy general] threw twenty-four flying swords at her consecutively but they were all reduced to ash just as before.... When the five Celestials of the Crane saw three of their compatriots captured, they decided to flee on their cranes. Who would have known, however, that the five cranes have all been injured by the 'blood light' ... the five celestials finally have to use their ability to travel underground to make their escape.[39]

The red light or 'blood light' that saves the day is, in fact, the blood, the 'pollutant'[40] produced during birth. *Warriors of the Yang Family* contains a similar case. Here the 'blood force' emanating from the birth fluids of a female warrior actually destroys the celestial opponent as he tries to escape by transforming himself into a stream of light. [41]

That birth fluids, pollutants considered dirty and associated with the female, can be considered the most powerful
weapon against evil celestials and magical weapons, demonstrates
again the need for *yin* to destroy evil.

Unlike most Chinese fiction, which shows strong misogy-
nistic tendencies, women warriors are celebrated in *Three Tales
from the Tang, Warriors of the Yang Family* and *Female Celestial*. Even if some are consumed with passion and amoral in their
pursuit of love, they are all brave and intelligent. They are
superior in military might and more faithful and upright than the
men who, though espousing Confucian principles, stoop to
expediency, lie and cheat.

This affirmation and even aggrandizement of female
power may be seen as being subversive to the dominant patriarchal culture. But, in fact, most of it is not. With the exception of
Female Celestial, women warriors serve the Chinese state and
their Chinese mates. Aside from making their own decisions
concerning marriage partners, which may necessitate betrayal of
their own families and states, they adhere firmly to the principles
of Confucianism and are model 'Chinese' heroines.

The only positive recognition of powers of the *yin* lies in
the Qing novel, *Female Celestial*. Considered a 'great new
wonder' (*xinda qishu*)[42] soon after it was published in 1711,
Female Celestial traces the career of a historical rebel female
religious cult leader, Tang Saier.

In this 100 chapter novel, Tang Saier is a reincarnation of
the goddess of the moon (Chang O) destined to lead an army
against the reigning emperor, an enemy made in heaven during
her previous incarnation. She gains legitimacy by claiming to
support the ex-emperor whose throne had been usurped, although
she never does find him. In the meantime, she becomes the
general of a formidable army staffed by numerous women
warriors and rules a court in which the female reigns supreme.
She finally returns to heaven after the death of her enemy.

The novel is noteworthy and exceptional not only in its affirmation of the *yin* but also in its implication that evil is frequently necessary for implementing that which is good. There is something topsy-turvy about the entire book when examined from a patriarchal, Confucian point of view. It makes use of Confucian ideals to justify the rebel movement and many of the actions carried out, but it inverts so many traditional concepts concerning gender and morality that *Female Celestial* basically subverts orthodox culture. It examines the rebellion of a female cult leader from the cult's point of view.

As a reincarnation of the goddess of the moon, a reigning symbol of the world of darkness, Tang Saier represents the force of *yin* herself. One of her appellations is Mistress of the Moon (*yuejun*). She champions a woman's world in which the female is more valuable and powerful than the male. Before she is born, her mother dreams of the child-bearing goddess of a local temple handing her a baby. When she asks whether it is a boy or a girl, the goddess replies, "A girl is better than a boy."[43] Before the middle of the book, not only is the traditional preference for male children subverted, but male dominance is also annihilated. After subduing a male warrior and a man noted for his inordinate strength, the swordswoman Gongsun announces, "You ought to know, it is now a woman's world!"[44]

Other military romances manifest the need for the *yin* to protect the *yang*; *Female Celestial* proceeds a step further in asserting the superiority of the *yin* over the *yang*. Tang Saier is not only a female warrior, she is a generalissimo and referred to as a 'Saintly Queen,' an 'Imperial Priestess,' and a 'Female Emperor.' She uses the royal 'we' (*gujia*) when referring to herself and is suspected of harboring imperial ambitions.[45] Although she flies the banner of the usurped emperor, the fact is that she is the ruler of her armies and their conquered realm. When she orders an old maid to prostrate herself before the ancestral tablet of her deceased husband, the unwilling maid chants,

The husband is a ghost of an untimely death,
The wife now reigns as an emperor.[46]

She is predestined to wield military power and rise higher in status
than a mere queen.[47] Even one of her followers claims that she
is no different from an emperor.[48]

While the might of female warriors manifests the triumph
of the *yin* over the *yang*, their dependence on magic for military
strength underscores its impossibility in real life. In fact, the
imagined power of women may have been inversely proportional
to the social and physical restraints suffered by women during the
Ming and the Qing. The female warrior is ultimately a figment
of the imagination and a product of its patriarchal culture.
Although the figure of the woman warrior affirms female power,
this power must serve the dominant male society. More signifi-
cantly, one sees through these ravishing beauties reflections of the
desires and fantasies of its male readers. Armed with supernatural
powers, the woman warrior is not only a helpful mate but is also
barbarically passionate. She seems to fill a void in real life. The
continued appeal of the female warrior after the proliferation of
the traditional novels discussed (in the Peking opera, local
dramas, films, *kung-fu* novels and more recently in T.V. series)
seem also to attest to the enduring attraction of the power, magic
and passion embodied in her.

Notes

1.   Belonging to this category are all the stories heard and films
     seen during her childhood by the modern Chinese American
     writer, Maxine Hong. See Maxine Hong Kingston, *The
     Women Warrior: Memoirs of a Girlhood Among Ghosts*,
     (New York: Alfred A. Knopf, 1984), 19.

2. Chu Renhuo, *Sui Tang yanyi* (Hong Kong: Xuelin Shudian, 1974). The author lived from ca. 1630 to ca. 1705.

3. Qian Cai and Jun Feng, *Sho Yue quanzhuan* (Hong Kong: Xiangji shuju, no date). My edition was renamed *Jingzhong Yuezhuan*). The authors lived in the early Qing period.

4. Lu Xixing, *Fengshen yanyi* (Hong Kong: Zhonghua shuju, 1985). The author lived between 1520 and ca. 1601. This novel has traditionally been attributed to Xü Zhonglin but Liu Ts'un-yan has proven it more likely to be Lu Xixing. See Liu Ts'un-yan, *Buddhist and Taoist Influences on Chinese Novels*, vol. 1 (Wiesbaden: Kommissionsverlag, 1962).

5. Lu Xixing 53:505.

6. Xiong Damu, *Yangjiajiang yanyi* (Beijing: Baowentang shudian, 1986). The author lived in the 16th century. The original title was *BeiSong zhizhuan*.

7. Rulian Jüshi, ed., *Shuo Tang Sanzhuan*, (Beijing: Baowentang shudian, 1987). The editor lived in the late 18th century.

8. Lüxiong, *Nüxian waishi* (Tianjin: Baihua wenyi chubanshe, 1984). The author lived from ca. 1640 to ca. 1722.

9. Lüxiong 32:365.

10. Celestials, be they good or evil, are all considered Daoist immortals. Although all Daoist immortals are presumed 'good,' the distinction between them and evil spirits in the form of wayward celestials is often bleary.

11. How such animals attained the *dao* is not clear. One method was absorption of the essence of nature for an inordinate length of time; another was conscious abstinence and self-cultivation.

12. Rulian Jüshi 34:190-1.

13. A famous beauty of the Warring States period (403-221 B.C.). Her name has become synonymous with beauty itself.

14. Another famous beauty of the Han dynasty. A consort in the imperial harem, this Chinese princess volunteered to marry a foreign chieftain, much to the regret of the Emperor Yuandi (48-32 B.C.) when he got to meet her for the first time during the farewell banquet.

15. The goddess of the moon is considered the most beautiful celestial being.

16. Reflecting the traditional standard of beauty, all the ravishing women warriors in Chinese fiction, even the foreign ones, are blessed with tiny feet. Foot-binding has been a Chinese custom since the Song (960-1260).

17. Rulian Jüshi 45:257. Unlike swords, although also quite long, these combat knives are broad and are only sharpened on one edge.

18. Literally 'heavenly god,' he is a Daoist celestial who helps a barbarian army against the Chinese. By implication, all celestials helping enemies of the protagonists are evil.

19. Xiong Damu 49:252.

20. Lu Xixing 44:407.

21. Xiong Damu 33:174-5.

22. For more information on the formations, see C.T. Hsia, "The Military Romance," ed. Cyril Birch, *Studies in Chinese Literary Genres* (Berkeley: University of California Press, 1974), 352-357. The article has been indispensable for this study. I did not read all the books discussed by Hsia, but I have added four works: *The Yufei Saga*; *Female Celestial*; *Traces of Immortals in the Wilderness*; and *Wounds of Romance*.

23. In *The Yufei Saga* (120), for example, warriors Meng Banjie and Tang Huai combat two sisters over a deer, eventually meet their father and are offered the hands of these maidens.

24. Since parental consent is necessary for the legitimation of any marriage, agreement to marriage on the woman's part implies willingness to let her parents know that she has been compromised; they are thus forced to give their consent. Both Han Qilong and Niu Tong procured their wives by capturing and raping these attractive opponents. Qian Cai and Jun Feng 97-98; 100.

25. This appreciation of effeminate beauty in men reflects the taste in traditional Chinese society; by then, it had endorsed civil achievement over military valor.

26. A Six Dynasties figure famous for his effeminate handsomeness.

27. Northern foreigners referred to by the Chinese as barbarians, *fan*, call the Chinese, southern barbarians, *man*.

28. Qian Cai and Jun Feng 78:141.

29. Rulian Jüshi 17:98.

30. Xiong Damu 36:195.

31. Xiong Damu 42:221.

32. Rulian Jüshi 52:296-7.

33. Qian Cai and Jun Feng 78:141-2.

34. Xiong Damu 35:186 to 36; 191.

35. Rulian Jüshi 27:147-8.

36. Rulian Jüshi 98-102.

37. For more examples of infatuated foreign princesses, see
     C.T. Hsia 376-378.

38. Lao Tzu, *Tao Te Ching*, D.C. Lau, trans. (Harmondsworth,
     Eng.: Penguin, 1963), 62.

39. Rulian Jüshi 35:302-3.

40. According to Emily M. Ahern, "The defining characteristic
     of a polluting substance in Chinese society is that it prevents
     those who come in contact with it from associating with the
     gods." The gods obviously encompass all sorts of spirits
     and supernatural beings. "The prohibition is most rigorous
     for those who come into closest contact with birth fluids."
     See Emily Ahern, "The Power and Pollution of Chinese
     Women," ed. Margery Wolf and Roxane Witke, *Women in
     Chinese Society* (Stanford, California: Stanford University
     Press, 1975), 202.

41. Lu Xixing 37:196-7.

42. Yang Zhongxian, "The Editor's Introduction (Xiaodian shuoming)" in Lü Xiong, *Nüxian waishi* (Tianjin: Baihua wenyi chubanshe, 1985) 9.

43. Lüxiong 2:15.

44. Lüxiong 36:412.

45. Lüxiong 55:633-4.

46. Lüxiong 47:534.

47. Lüxiong 2:17.

48. Lüxiong 85:943.

THE FEMALE HERO IN THE ISLAMIC
RELIGIOUS TRADITION

Marcia K. Hermansen

The study of the image of the heroic woman illuminates both the role of gender in the symbolization of religious traditions and the effect that this has on women's lives. In particular, studying the case of the Islamic religious tradition provides comparative material on the distinctive contours of the image of women as symbolized in the cultural imagination. This enables one to trace historical shifts in the modes of formulating these images and discloses ethnocentric assumptions about gender categories. It also provides data and suggestions for women's participation in revisioning their past and choosing how to integrate it in shaping their future.

The precise definition of the heroic proves to be somewhat elusive, especially for moderns. Certain authors speak of a "desacralization" of the earlier concept of mythic heroes in which heroes become any "historical person of mettle" or even public celebrities.[1] The traditional formulations of the heroic role focus on the mythic dimension of the heroic quest that are expressed in a narrative style in which there is a plot/quest itinerary. For example, earlier studies by V. Propp, F. Raglan, S. Freud, C. Jung and J. Campbell[2] see the hero as someone whose quest follows an archetypal pattern or at least a formal set of rules. More extended psychological analyses of the heroic mode suggest a process within cultural and religious traditions in which individuals identify with the hero. The heroic motif is then available to assist them with their own integration through a healing or transformative function. Hence the role of the hero is to confront and overcome crisis and alienation as he is reintegrated into the society to which he brings at the same time a transforming gift. Today there are explorations of the heroic quest motif suggesting that literature which takes a woman's perspective might offer a different view of the quest.[3] For example, by examining the role of the heroic female in modern literature, C. Pearson and K. Pope suggest that the qualities of contemporary female heroes include the promise of a more complete transformation of society, the suggestion that previously forbidden qualities must be assimilated into the self, and the learning of a series of paradoxical truths by journeying through duality.[4] A related observation on sexual difference in the appropriation of symbols is that

> ... men and women of a single tradition — when working with the same symbols and myths, writing in the same genre, and living in the same religious or professional circumstances — display certain consistent male/female differences in using symbols. Women's symbols and myths tend to build from biological experiences; men's symbols and myths tend to invert them. Women's mode of using symbols seems given to the muting of opposition, contradiction, inversion, and conversion. Women's myths and rituals tend to explore a state of being; men's tend to build elaborate and discrete stages between self and other.[5]

The pursuit of classical "sacralized" heroes, much less heroines, in the classical Islamic textual tradition is not an easy task. One is dogged by the implicitly denigrating suggestions that Islam lacks a true mythic imagination because it was "born and matured in the full light of history."[6] We may detect in such formulations the lingering specter of a literalist, concrete and atomistic "Semitic mind" that offers less scope for a truly mythic imagination. A similar case has been made for Hebrew Biblical narrative; one scholar contends that only the story of Job is truly evocative of the heroic paradigm.[7]

A further task confronting us is to differentiate between the paradigmatic and the heroic. I postulate that the paradigmatic establishes a model or set of qualities to be fulfilled by subsequent persons. For example, in the Islamic tradition the idea of specific qualities of piousness or generosity could be construed as paradigmatic, while the broader concept of the "sunna" or the reported teachings and actions of the Prophet Muhammad that come to function as normative for Muslims could be seen as constituting a fuller articulation of the paradigm. According to D. Capps and F. Reynolds, a biographical process inevitably takes place in the development of religious tradition in which the historical elements of individual lives interact with previously established exemplary paradigms, being shaped by them and instantiating them in popular imagination, narration, and life itself.[8] The conceptual scope of the paradigmatic therefore is less specific than that of the heroic. While the paradigmatic suggests the control and reinforcement of tradition and the cultural status quo, the heroic, and especially the female heroic, often represent a challenge to established tradition that signals the existence of a cultural critique.

In terms of feminist theory, culling the past for exceptional women who defy the oppressiveness of tradition may, in fact, not be a particularly productive enterprise. If one can find a handful of token women warriors or religious scholars, does this somehow prove that the Islamic tradition provides more paradigmatic or heroic scope for women than other comparable traditions? For example, it has been shown that the availability of such paradigms through religious symbols that positively value the feminine, goddesses, or female role models does not necessarily imply a correlation with the improved socio-historical status of women in a given tradition.[9] The study of paradigmatic women in religious tradition, I would argue, is instructive heuristically, because it discloses the contours of how ordinary lives should be lived. The paradigmatic role is also fulfilled by a number of heroic women. At the same time the study of heroic women who are exceptions to the norm raises the much broader issue of the challenge to the cultural and religious status quo.

Overall, heroic women have received less attention from the scholars of hero myths. Why is this? At the most basic level the heroine appears less frequently than the hero. While it is obvious that male authors of classical texts identified more with male protagonists, an additional factor in this imbalance seems to be that it was more disturbing for women to have the status-challenging role of the hero. After all, women's roles, in so far as these have been viewed as embodying the natural order, may themselves function as symbols that reinforce traditional cultural norms. For scholars of the heroic motif, heroines have been more difficult to type and thus resist closure even more than male heroes. An additional feature of the Islamic materials, which may complicate our task, is the fact that most classical narrative in Islamic civilization, particularly that written in Arabic, does not feature plot development in the classic Aristotelian sense. It is, therefore, more difficult to locate individuals whose life stories embody the sacral hero cycle especially in the original anecdotal form of these accounts. Finally, the early biographical tradition in Islam focused less on the exceptional individual than on the community as a whole and the human relationships within it. Hamilton Gibb writes,

> ... the conception that underlies the older biographical dictionaries is that the history of the Islamic Community is essentially the contribution of individual men and women to the building up and transmission of its specific culture. That is, it is these persons (rather than the political governors) who represent or reflect the active force of Muslim society in their respective

spheres; and that their individual contributions are worthy of being recorded for future generations.[10]

The writers of the early biographical compendia were thus not memorializing paradigmatic or even exceptional individuals but rather establishing the paradigm of the community. As a result, there is usually no commentary in which the compiler points out that certain individual acts are noteworthy or exceptional. Mentioning them is stylistically sufficient in this genre. In fact, the majority of biographical notices in classical Islamic sources do not feature character or plot development but rather present a series of quotations and anecdotes related to the individual or topic under consideration.

This study of the female hero in the Islamic tradition will focus on gender, culture, and historical period.

1)   Gender — Female as Distinct from Male in the Heroic Paradigm

An overview of female heroic types in the Islamic tradition suggests the following categories: wife and mother, warrior, and spiritual virtuoso.

Wife and mother

The first follower of the Prophet was his wife, Khadīja, who is portrayed as wise, competent, patient, brave, and a constant support to her husband. Interestingly, there are relatively few anecdotes that detail her activities more precisely, although she is featured in folk accounts of the Prophet's life.

'Ā'isha was the wife who was closest to the prophet among those he married after Khadīja's death. She was regarded, as were his other wives, as one of the "Mothers of the

Believers." Respected as a transmitter of many of his sayings or ḥadīth reports, she was also considered as one of the Companions who possessed particular legal acumen and was accorded the title of "faqīh" (jurist). In fact, there is a report that the Prophet recognized 'Ā'isha's impotance by saying, "Draw a part of your religion from little al-ḥumayra."[11]   After the death of the Prophet, she became involved in the struggle for succession, most notably in opposing the rule of the fourth caliph, 'Alī. At the Battle of the Camel, 'Ā'isha urged on the opponents of 'Alī from the back of her camel, hence the name of this encounter. After the defeat of her faction, she agreed to retire from active political life. 'Ā'isha is a heroic figure from the standpoint of Sunni Islam. Her life is presently receiving closer attention as a potential role model for activist Muslim women. For example, a contemporary Sunni commentator writes,

> Ayesha was a teacher of men and women. In turn her students, men and women, taught others how to govern, how to organize Muslim communities, and how to arrange Muslim family and social life. The holy Prophet bore witness to Ayesha's intellect, understanding, rational approach to life. At a time of crisis she had no hesitation in taking over command of the Islamic army and directing it in the field of battle. In peacetime she gave religious rulings and helped the most learned of the Companions of the Prophet differentiate between right and wrong.

> Women like the sublime Ayesha can emerge in an Islamic society if women are taught right from the beginning to take responsibilities in the life of the community. Women must prepare for the main goal of the Muslim community: JIHĀD.... The Qur'ān teaches that believing men and women are

"from each other" and partners in all aspects of
the Islamic struggle, even to the extent of hijrah
and qitāl (armed struggle) (See Qur'ān 3:195).
But modern Muslims believe that women should
be excluded from even the most elementary deci-
sion-making processes.

The author concludes by suggesting that Muslims should begin
commemorating Ā'isha's life and role and even "start holding
formal ceremonies to show respect" for her.[12]

Fāṭima, the daughter of the Prophet, was one of the major
figures in the classical Islamic religious tradition. Her role was
especially elaborated in the Shi'ī tradition where she was featured
as the only female among the "fourteen pure ones,"[13] the suffering mother of the martyred grandsons of the Prophet, and the wife
of the heroic 'Alī. Her role has been traditionally described as
subdued, focusing on motherhood, loyalty, sorrow, and long-suffering patience. As a symbol of female religiosity, she has been
noted her for piety, for receiving guidance from the prophet and
revelations from angels, and for serving as an intercessor for the
faithful. She is counted among the four greatest women in
history[14] and is sometimes characterized as lacking the female
"defiency" of menstruation so that she can always fulfill the
religious duties of prayer and fasting.[15] The contemporary
Iranian writer, 'Alī Sharī'atī portrays her as an existential
heroine who is "herself" rather than subordinate to, or definable
in terms of, others.[16]

The value of Mary lies with Jesus Christ whom
she delivered and nourished. The value of
Assiyeh, the wife of Pharaoh, lies with Moses,
whom she nourished and befriended. The value of
Khadijeh lies with Mohammad whom she
befriended and with Fatima whom she gave birth
to and nourished.

And the value of Fatima? What can I say? To
whom does her value belong? To Khadijeh? To
Mohammad? To Ali? To Hosein? To Zainab?[17]
To herself!![18]

The normative Islamic tradition represented by the ḥadīth
honors traits of motherhood as indicated in the Prophet's state-
ments such as, "Paradise lies at the feet of mothers." The
maternal role, which includes the dimension of suffering, is
elevated to an even more heroic status as evidenced by certain
ḥadīth reports that accord the mother, who dies in childbirth or
loses her child, the status of a martyr.[19]

Warrior

A number of first generation Muslims known as the
Companions of the Prophet were women warriors. Many of them
are memorialized in the final volume of Ibn Sa'd's *Tabaqāt*, a
tenth-century biographical compendium of which the last volume
is entirely devoted to biographies of women. This source forms
the basis for many later accounts of early Muslim women.
Typical of this group is the doughty Umm 'Umāra who was
wounded repeatedly in battle and stood alone in defending the
prophet as others fled the battlefield at Uḥud, believing that he
had been slain. As reported in Ibn Sa'd, "Umm 'Umāra was
wounded twelve times at Uḥud and her hand was cut off."[20]
She was married three times and had children from each marriage. While conservative Muslim male authorities argue that
women can only participate in the jihād as nurses, cooks, and care
takers, these early accounts clearly indicate the active presence of
women in early battles.

Women were certainly not excluded from the ranks of
martyrs and warriors in early Islamic history although later
emphasis on the propriety of their seclusion made it more difficult

for these early roles to be acknowledged. In fact, the first person said to have "suffered for the faith" was a female martyr, Summaya, daughter of Khubbāṭ. According to Ibn Saʿd's biographical entry, she accepted Islam early in Makka. She suffered for her religion at the hands of those who wanted her to abjure her faith but she held steadfast and was patient. One day, Abū Jahl, a staunch enemy of the Prophet and Islam, passed by her and stabbed her in the forehead causing her death. Although she was already aged and weak, she was the first to die for her faith. On the day of the battle of Badr, when Abū Jahl was killed, the Prophet said to her son, 'Ammār ibn Yāsir, "God has slain your mother's murderer." Famous companions of the Prophet such as Mujāhid have called her "the first martyr of Islam."[21]

Another warrior was one of the Prophet's paternal aunts, Ṣafiyya, daughter of 'Abd al-Muṭṭalib, who killed a spy with a tent peg while her male guard hesitated out of fear. She later participated as a combatant in the battle of Uḥud. Another of his aunts, 'Ātika, had a dream that predicted the defeat of the Quraish at the hands of the Prophet. This prompted the Prophet's enemy Abū Jahl to make the following sarcastic comment, "O children of 'Abd al-Muṭṭalib, isn't it enough for you that your men are prophets without your women becoming prophets also?"[22]

In the contemporary period, it has become common for authors — even conservative authors — to dedicate a section of their works (sometimes even whole volumes) to the role of women in Islam. Depending on their position regarding normative roles for women today, such authors may include examples of women participating in battles. On the one hand, Syed Sulaimān Nadvī, a well-known traditional scholar from India, mentions a number of instances where women actually took part in armed combat. In his account of women's heroic deeds, the story of Umm 'Umāra is followed by accounts of the military exploits of Muslim women at the battles of Qadisiya, Maisān, Damascus, and Yarmūk where "the women of Quraish flung forward with swords flashing in the battle until they were ahead of their men."[23]   According to another account, a Muslim heroine, Umm Abān, avenged her husband 'Otba's death by taking his bow and arrow and killing non-Muslim enemies including his murderer Tuma, governor of Damascus.[24] Among the other early Muslim heroines mentioned is Asmā', daughter of the Caliph Abu Bakr, who always fought side by side with her husband on horseback.[25] In the latter part of his survey, Nadvī mentions Muslim queens and warriors of India as ranking among the heroic Muslim women. On the other hand, the more conservative author of *The Stories of the Sahaabah* (Companions of the Prophet), Muḥammad Zakariyya Kaandhlawī, mentions a number of the same women in a chapter on "Women's Courage and Spirit for Islam" but limits the account of their activities to tending the wounded and omits any mention of combat.[26] Such a process of "editing" may also be found in the romances of medieval France, where the few heroines who were also warriors and thus defied cultural expectations were portrayed as the quintessential "other" — "the Saracen" — who had been domesticated by conversion and marriage to a Frenchman.[27] Joan of Arc, perhaps the sole exception, was made "other" by symbols of her sexual ambiguity such as cross- dressing.[28]

In classical Islam, as we have noted, numerous women fought in the early military campaigns; their exploits are recounted as exceptional in classical biographical compendia such as the *Tabaqāt* of Ibn Sa'd. This should not be overlooked as an example in which a feature of religious history (the fact that women fought as warriors in early Islamic history) and ideology (that armed struggle in the path of God is condoned and even exhorted by the religion) provides a different paradigm for operating in a cultural imagination. While there is no need to represent the female warrior as culturally "other" in the Islamic popular imagination, there is also no particular abundance of the female warrior motif. However, it is found in folk-epics such as the Persian *Shāh Nāmeh*[29] and the Arabic *Banī Hilāl*[30] in which women play romantic, queenly, and occasionally military roles.

In terms of the theme, Persian poetic romances feature the motif of the local hero being challenged by a foreign princess whom he later marries.   Here "otherness" is resolved through the assimilative function of the heroine to whom marriage symbolizes the formation of new political and cultural alliances. In terms of the heroine as a mediator, a study of Bedouin heroic narrative concludes that while "the heroines usually exhibit courage in battle equal to their male conterparts, ... they possess in addition a measure of wisdom that balances the male tendency to swift and sometimes precipitous action."[31]

Women's participation in armed struggle in the early history of Islam signals something significant about the times. As in other religious traditions, the scope of women's participation during the early period seems to have been much broader than when the institutions and standards of the community became more established. The fact that the process of jihād or struggle to establish the faith occurred so early in the formation of the Islamic tradition may help to explain women's participation as warriors in this tradition.

While women's participation in revolutionary and liberation movements in the modern period signals a similar upheaval in the social and political status quo, it has not necessarily guaranteed a permanent improvement in their situation as in the well-known cases of the Algerian and Iranian revolutions.[32] In her study on modern Lebanese women writers and the civil war in Lebanon, Miriam Cooke traces the changing dynamic of women's role in war. In this case, women have gone from being cheerleaders, sandwich makers, and nurses to being voices of conscience in the midst of the war experience.[33] The fact that women can be soldiers may be less telling about improvements in women's status than the fact that women's voices are raised about the experience of war itself. As feminist studies on the ideology of war tell us, the whole experience of belligerence and conflict does not necessarily indicate the direction women should take.

Heroines have also embodied the sense of defiance and outrageousness in Muslim history. Before she became Muslim, the colorful Hind, wife of the Makkan leader Abū Sufyān, was a major enemy of the Prophet. She arranged the slaying of the Muslim hero, Ḥamza (uncle of the Prophet) and ate his liver raw on the battlefield. She performed songs and dances among the bodies of the dead Muslims at the battle of Uḥud. The following verses are attributed to her,

> We are daughters of the morning star,
> We trample cushions underfoot,
> Our necks are adorned with pearls,
> Our hair is perfumed with musk,
> If you battle us, we will crush you in our arms,
> If you retreat we will let you go.
> Farewell to love.[34]

As Fatima Mernissi observes regarding these verses,

> One of women's roles in Pre-Islamic Arabia was to spur men on during war to fight to the end, to not flinch, to brave death on the battle field. This role obviously has nothing to do with the image of the nurturing woman who bandages wounds and comforts the dying. Hind and her war song expresses, on the contrary, an image of woman as exhorter to death.[35]

In another poem, cited in one of the earliest biographies of the Prophet, Hind speaks the lines,

> Let us fall on Yathrib (Madīna) with an over-
> whelming attack,
> With horses kept hard by,
> Every long-bodied charger.[36]

Hind is not simply a woman warrior, but a warrior opposed to Islam. Even in her ultimate capitulation to Islam, she remains defiant.

An interesting transformation of the story of Hind and Hamza in the form of an oral folk narrative is recounted by Jan Knappert.[37] In this variant Hamza is killed by a wicked witch (at some level a transformation of Hind). Hamza is married to a female jinn (spirit) and with her has a daughter called Qurayshī. After her father's death, the daughter searches the earth with an army of female jinns and ultimately captures his murderess, the witch, who then accepts Islam and repents of her evil deeds. At this event, all assembled are shown a vision of Hamza and the other martyrs in Paradise. The Prophet tells Qurayshī, "Your father, Hamza, would not enjoy this new existence if he had not died," and thus Qurayshī is reconciled with her father's murderess. This variant is noteworthy both for the prominence of its female characters and for the assimilative and mediating function of the female hero illustrated in it.

Another notable example of an outrageous and defiant heroine is Sukayna, daughter of the Prophet's grandson, Husayn. Her story is among those recently recovered by the Muslim feminist, Fatima Mernissi.

> Sukayna was born in the year 49 of the Hejira (about A.D. 671). She was celebrated for her beauty — an explosive mixture of physical attractiveness, critical intelligence, and caustic wit. The most powerful men debated with her; caliphs and princes proposed marriage to her, which she disdained for political reasons. Nevertheless, she ended up marrying five, some say six, husbands. She quarreled with some of them, made passionate declarations of love to others, brought one to court for infidelity, and never pledged ṭā'a (obedience, the key principle of Muslim marriage) to any of

them. In her marriage contracts she stipulated that she would not obey her husband, but would do as she pleased, and that she did not acknowledge that her husband had the right to practice polygyny. All this was the result of her interest in political affairs and poetry. She continued to receive visits from poets, and despite her several marriages, to attend the meetings of the Quraish tribal council, the equivalent of today's democratic municipal councils. Her personality has fascinated the historians who have devoted pages and pages, sometimes whole biographies to her.... She made one of her husbands sign a marriage contract that officially specified her right to nushūz, that rebellion against marital control that so tormented the fuqaha. She claimed the right to be nāshiz, and paraded it, like her beauty and her talent, to assert the importance and vitality of women in the Arab tradition.[38]

Spiritual Virtuoso

Rābi'a of Baṣra (d. 801) and other female Sufis represent this category. Rābi'a, the most prominent female Sufi, may be seen as representing the mythic aspect of the heroine most fully since the account of her life features the itinerary of a quest.

Rābi'a is one of the best-known women in the Islamic tradition and was the subject of a study done by the British scholar Margaret Smith in the 1920s.[39] Her story continues to appeal to many; a number of books and even an Arabic feature film have memorialized her life. One finds entries on her in most of the standard Sufi hagiographies, although not all such works offer anything resembling a complete heroic cycle. I have chosen to use her as an example because there is more narrative material about her. What draws me to her story is a troubling sense that is sometimes appealing and sometimes disturbing. Even today the redaction of 'Aṭṭār, made some four hundred years after her death, has an odd sense of non-closure — a sense that there is some further mystery to be penetrated.

Let me begin by reviewing some of the formal motifs of the hero cycle as outlined by V. Propp, F. Raglan, J. Campbell, and others. These are portents before birth, loss of parents, separation from society, quest, resolution, attainment of goal, and return to society. In Rābi'a's story, we find enough material for tracing some basic life stages — birth, youth, adulthood and death. In addition, a number of anecdotes about her sayings and activities have been preserved.

Birth

In an anecdote set on the night of her birth, the following account is related:

> He [her father] then fell asleep, deeply grieved and heavy-hearted, and Muḥammad the Prophet [may the peace of God rest upon him] appeared to him in a dream, saying, "Do not be grieved. You have been blessed with a daughter who will be a great saint; her intercession will be wished for by seventy thousand of my community.[40]

Initiation

According to Campbell, the archetypal journey of the hero proceeds through three stages: departure, initiation, and return.[41] It is, however, not quite so precise in the Rābi'a cycle; perhaps her initiation could best be represented by a childhood experience in which she seems to rebuke God. As a young orphaned slave-girl, she is being chased by a stranger when she falls down and breaks her wrist. At this point she says to God,

> "O God, I am a stranger without father or mother; I have been sold in bondage, and now my wrist is broken. But despite all this, I am not distressed about anything which has befallen me. I only wish you to be content, so that I might know if I have gained your satisfaction or not." She then heard an unseen voice tell her, "Do not mourn, for in the hereafter you will reach such a rank that even those nearest to God in heaven will be proud of your station."[42]

This seems to mark the beginning of her intense relationship to God. In terms of return, she spends her whole life in a quest during which she is repeatedly tested. She does benefit her society through example and teaching. Unlike the male hero, she is not fully reintegrated into society, and thus she remains celibate and a virtual hermit.

Quest and Travel — Pilgrimage

A recurring theme in the Rābi'a anecdotes is pilgrimage. One of the most startling anecdotes is the following, of which I will suggest a number of possible interpretations.

> According to Shaikh Farmādī, Rābi'a crawled on her side for seven years until she reached Mt. 'Arafāt. Once there an unseen voice censured her, "You imposter, what is all this quest you are preoccupied with? If you desire Me, then I will show you one flash of my glory and consume

you." Rābi'a then entreated: "O Lord of Majesty, Rābi'a lacks such capacity, but I yearn for the essence of spiritual poverty (faqr)." The voice responded, "O Rābi'a, Poverty is the scourge of Our Wrath, which we placed on the Saints' path. When less than a hair's width remains between them and our union, We turn their affairs topsy-turvy and cast them into bereavement. Yet you are still enthralled by seventy thousand veils of your own day and age. Only when you emerge from beneath these veils and step firmly upon the Way will you be worthy to profess that poverty. If not, then look up." As she lifted her eyes, she beheld an ocean of blood, suspended in midair.

The same invisible voice recounted, "Those lovers who perished in their search before attaining to the first way-station of Union with us — this Ocean is the blood of their hearts. In neither world and in no stage of the Way is any name or indication to be found of them."

"O Almighty Lord, allow me to view but a token of the grace they have attained," Rābi'a be-seeched. Instantaneously, Rābi'a began to men-struate. "The primary stage of their way" the voice answered, "is that they crawl on their sides for seven years to render homage to an earthen clod; however, We deny them access to their goal by reason of themselves." Rābi'a became in-flamed upon hearing this. "Lord," she cried, "You neither grant me entry into your mansion nor permit me to rest in my own house in Baṣra. Either let me into Your house in Makka or leave me home in Baṣra. Once, so deep was my yearn-

ing for You, that I wouldn't even presume to
approach your house. Now I do not even merit
entrance." So saying, Rābi'a turned back to Baṣra
and remained secluded in her home.[43]

The menstruation taboo is very striking here. It resonates
with the motif of wounding as discussed by Pearson[44] in which
traditional women heroes experienced themselves as wounded in
the same way that the fisher king is wounded in the grail myth.
'Aṭṭār, in a poetic version in the *Conference of the Birds*, under-
stands menstruation as a symbol of her being distracted by "waves
of sentient success or failure."[45] In a version of the same story
originally attributed to Shaikh Farmādī (ca.1084), the focus is
shifted to the insignificance of her apparent goal, the Ka'ba, "an
earthen clod,"[46] and her ultimate return to her home in Baṣra.
As a corroboration of this interpretation, we find that in a number
of other pilgrimage narratives of Rābi'a, the Ka'ba is portrayed
as leaving its position to come to her, so that, for example, the
famous male Sufi, Ibrāhīm Ibn Adham, was unable to visit it at
that time.[47] A further example is the following quotation in
which she minimizes the significance of pilgrimage to a physical
place:

> O God my heart is heavy with sorrow. Where am
> I going to? I am but a handful of dirt and your
> house is only a stone. You are my sole desire.[48]

Is the message the fact that the goal is to be pursued within
irrespective of gender? Or is it that her menstruation is a symbol
of spiritual attainment, since it is associated with "the blood of the
hearts of the martyr gnostics" as "a token of the grace they have
attained?"[49] My point is that this narrative is not paradigmatic
but heroic, and surprisingly evocative of modern senses of non-
closure and struggle (whether one wants to read it in Sufi terms of

struggle against illusion or in feminist terms of struggle against patriarchal oppression).

Gender Ambiguity

One element of Rābi'a's story distinctive from that of male Sufi seekers is that of sexual ambiguity. Comments and anecdotes regarding her "maleness" are quite common in the hagiographic texts.

> Her perfection and the virtues of her soul evolved far beyond many of the later Sufi saints making her renowned as the "Crown of Men" (Tāj al-Rijāl);

> "No she wasn't a single woman
> But a hundred men over" ('Aṭṭār).[50]

Jāmī cites the following Arabic poem in the introduction to Rābi'a's biographical notice:

> If women were like the ones we mentioned,
> They would be preferred over men

> For the noun "the sun" being feminine is no disgrace
> And being masculine gendered is not the pride of "the Moon."[51]

In other words, gender is as arbitrary a construct as linguistic usage in marking nouns and does not limit the essential nature of the gendered person.

If anyone asks "Why have you included Rabia in the ranks of men?" My answer is the Prophet himself said, "God does not regard your outward forms." The root of the matter is not form, but intention, as the Prophet said, "Humans will be raised up according to their intentions" ... When a woman becomes a man in the path of God she is man and one cannot any more call her a woman.[52]

I would summarize Rābi'a as a culture-critiquing female hero for the following reasons: as a Sufi she is free to defy the norms of the material culture. She does not marry and is portrayed as rejecting a number of proposals from both spiritually and materially endowed males. She has no desire for worldly achievement. The incident of her menstruation is a heroic element in her story, revealing in my opinion surrender (as a positive option) and heroism in the face of failure. At the same time, the prevalence of comments reflecting sexual ambiguity points out the problematic nature of her heroic role within the culture.

2) Cultural/Religious Distinctiveness

While the Hellenic and Western European materials have formed the basis of most works on the subject of heroism, the Islamic tradition has its own set of heroines and its own distinctive narrative forms and character development. One case study that brings this out contrasts the portrayal of pre-Islamic heroines mentioned in the Qur'ān with post-Islamic ones. If Muslims are more free to create heroic stories about pre-Islamic Quranic women such as Hagar, 'Āṣiyya (wife of Pharaoh), Zuleikha (who loves Joseph), and Mary, than about the wives of the Prophet, what does this tell us about Islamic internal norms for female heroic behavior?

The Islamic tradition contains a theory of comparative religion through its theory of progressive yet cumulative revelation, which incorporates and Islamicizes elements known to previous traditions so that they have a continued and elaborated Islamic life of their own. In terms of our interest in the Islamic heroine, pre-Islamic women such as Hagar, 'Āsiyya, Mary and Zuleikha could be considered in terms of what is distinctive about their role within Islam.

For example, Hagar is a potentially strong figure in the Islamic tradition. Alone after her dismissal by the jealous Sarah, she travels with her infant son, Ismā'īl to Arabia. There she heroically and desperately runs back and forth in search of water. Ironically, although Hagar's paradigmatic act of running between the hillocks of al-Ṣafā and al-Marwa (sa'y) is incorporated as part of the Ḥajj rituals, most authorities permit using a slower gait because running between these points is only used in reference to males. 'Alī Sharī'atī, the Iranian activist scholar and religious theorist who died in 1978, dedicates a section of his book on the Ḥajj[53] to the Hagar (Ḥajar) motif.

> Sa'y is a quest/search. It is a movement with an aim. It is depicted by running and hurrying.... You are acting as Ḥajar.[54]

> Here in sa'y you are to play the role of Ḥajar — a woman, a poor, belittled Ethiopian slave and maid for Sārā. These are all of her qualifications in the human social system — in the system of polytheism, but not in the system of montheism (tauḥīd)! This slave is the addresser of Allāh, the mother of the great prophets (the messengers of Allāh), and the representative of Allāh's loveliest and dearest creatures. In this show of Ḥajj, she is the first and

distinguished character. In the house of Allāh she
is the only woman — a mother.[55]

... However Ḥajar, the model of submission, did
not "sit quietly." Soon, she arose and all alone
tried to run from one dry mountain to the other
searching for water! Constantly searching, moving, and struggling, she decided to rely on herself,
her feet, her will and her mind. Ḥajar was a
responsible woman, a mother, in love, all alone,
wandering, searching, enduring pain, disturbed,
deprived of support, lacking shelter, homeless,
isolated from her society, classless, raceless, and
hopeless; yet despite all these drawbacks, she was
HOPEFUL![56]

Sharī'atī goes on to expand on the significance of Hagar's search
for water, which for him symbolizes material life on earth, the
relation of humankind to nature, and finding heaven in this world
and enjoying its fruit on the earth. Although he relies on binary
oppositions of male/female, spirit/matter, eastern/western, he
positively portrays the material side represented by Hagar as
active, determined and equally valuable and necessary.[57]

Zuleikha, a female character found in the Qur'ān and in
Islamic literature, is portrayed with the elaborate role of a
romantic heroine who is spiritually transformed through her
initially illicit passion for the Prophet Joseph and the consequent
shame and suffering. In Muslim tradition, Joseph's predominant
attribute is his physical beauty, which women find irresistible.
Thus, Zuleikha, although condemned for her plotting to seduce
the youth, is also somewhat justified (in the Quranic version she
invites the noble ladies of Egypt to view Joseph; they are so
overcome that they lose their sense of decorum and accidentally
cut themselves with the knives provided them to cut their
fruit).[58] In later Persian poetic versions, such as Jāmī (1492)

and subsequent folk versions, the story of Joseph and Zuleikah is continued. She becomes impoverished and ages while he rises to wealth and glory. They are both ultimately transformed in an encounter where he acknowledges his love for her despite her decline in looks and status; God miraculously restores her youth and beauty.[59]

Another example is 'Āṣiyya, the wife of the Pharaoh who opposes Moses. She heroically stands up against her husband; by first rescuing the child Moses and then accepting his teaching.

Within the Islamic tradition, there are further distinct sub-categories of the heroic woman envisioned in regional, elite, and sectarian (Sunni, Shi'i and Sufi) traditions. In terms of sub-traditional influence, I suggest that mainstream Sunni religious tradition has fewer mythic heroes in terms of the more restricted definition of the mythic hero/ine. This could be due to the historically reinforced mood of confidence in Sunnism where history has "gone right" and the community cannot agree on error.[60] In Sunni Islam, lives tend to reaffirm cultural values as suggested by Ira Lapidus' study of the concept of adulthood. His thesis is illustrated by the autobiographies of al-Ghazzālī (1111) and Ibn Khaldūn (1404), which feature periods of quest/questioning that are ultimately resolved in the reaffirmations of dominant cultural norms.[61]

Our principle locations for cultural critique through heroic quests are thus Shi'ism, Sufism, and modernism. In contemporary Western formulations of the function of heroic myths, the challenge to the status quo and future orientation is seen as extremely significant. Campbell writes that the hero "is the champion not of things become but of things becoming, the dragon to be slain by him (her) is precisely the monster of the status quo."[62] However, this element of the heroic as understood in the Western tradition may not carry over wholesale into the Islamic materials. While there is cultural critique, particularly in Shi'ism, Sufism and modernism, there is a reluctance to see the new as fully superseding or slaying the old. Well-known literary motifs reflecting this are the Rustam/Sohrāb story in which the father unknowingly slays the son (this neatly contrasts with the Oedipus motif).[63] In the famous romance of Laila/Majnūn, the tragedy of the deaths of the separated lovers resists becoming an appeal for socio/cultural change unlike the message derived from its Western counterpart, Romeo and Juliet. It is rather seen to be in the nature of things symbolized by the mourning of the desert animals over the desolate graves of the two lovers, united in death. These brief remarks suggest that the heroic in Islamic tradition is not totally congruent with the heroic as a Western category.

3) Historical — from the Mythic to the Modern

There seems to be a general sense among critics that the full-fledged mythic hero cycle is disappearing from contemporary Western culture and being watered down to its more ephemeral, less transformative manifestations. Is this to some extent paralleled by the heroic motifs — male and female — in other traditions? The developmental trajectory of the heroic motif in the case of the Islamic tradition needs to be further explored by looking at contemporary works. Some produced by Muslims attempt to reappropriate prominent women of the religious/cultural past as paradigmatic for Muslim women today (see, for example, portrayals of the Prophet's wife 'Ā'isha, by (1) Fatima Mernissi (an Islamic feminist);[64] (2) Kaukab Siddique (a male feminist fundamentalist!!); and (3) others (such as the traditional Indian Muslim ulema, Nadvī and Thanvī).

Other works relevant to this topic include: 'Alī Sharī'atī's *Fāṭima is Fāṭima*, a work by an Iranian modernist that seeks to recast the Prophet's daughter Fāṭima as an existential heroine; the more traditional biographical studies of early Muslim women (for example, Bint al-Shāṭi');[65] and the works of Fatima Mernissi, a Muslim feminist who seeks to recover those aspects

of women's roles in history supressed by the subsequent tradition.[66] The autobiography of Zaynab al-Ghazzālī, a contemporary Islamic activist in Egypt, has been studied as both saintly
and subversive by Miriam Cooke.[67] Ghazzālī's autobiography
uses expressions and motifs associated with traditional saintly
qualities of piety (e.g., patience in the face of adversity and
miracles and changes of heart wrought in others by the saint's
presence). While she advocates traditional roles and strict
adherence to Islamic norms for women, she herself subverts them
(1) by asserting to her husband that her commitment to the cause
of the Muslim Brotherhood will outweigh her commitment to
marital roles and (2) by her willingness to meet with men in order
to further the activities of the group. A further source is fiction
by Muslim women in the contemporary period. These writers
both expose the difficulties faced by real women and revise the
sphere of heroic female activity. This has been studied by Cooke
and Laila Ahmed. Cooke, for example, has studied anti-war
feminists in Lebanon.[68]

Overall, do contemporary formulations reflect a "watering
down" of the heroic women, or are they a more conscious
polemicizing of tradition? What are the positive or creative
developments as contemporary Muslims revise their views of the
heroine? These questions can only be answered after a more
detailed study has been done than is possible here. Contemporary
Muslims, both men and woman, seem to be concerned with the
search for the paradigmatic woman as an explicit construct. It is
also clear that in the current state of cultural tension in Muslim
societies, writers, both male and female, are paying more
attention to the women of history and attempting to reappropriate
them through biographical, historical, and creative writing. Is this
evocation of female roles due to the fact that women in general
symbolize nature and their bodies are symbolic ground from
which to argue a vision of culture as it should be? Is it because
Muslims feel that the construct of the female role is the most
salient distinguishing feature of their ideology from modernity/the

West? Perhaps the age of the mythic heroine has come to a close just as the mythic hero in the contemporary West seems to have disappeared. Perhaps the place to look for her heirs is in the modern literary imagination where her critiquing function continues in a new form.

Notes

1. Theodor E. Gaster, "Heroes," in *Encyclopedia of Religion* (New York: MacMillan, 1987), 6:304-5.

2. V. Propp, *Morphology of the Folktale* (Austin: University of Texas, 1968); F. Raglan, *The Hero* (London: Methuen and Co., 1936) and Joseph Campbell, *The Hero with a Thousand Faces* (New York: World Publishing Co., 1970).

3. See Carol Pearson and Katherine Pope, *The Female Hero in American and British Literature* (New York: R.R. Bowker, 1981) and Maureen Murdock, *The Heroine's Journey* (Boston: Shambhala, 1990).

4. Pearson and Pope, 14-15.

5. Caroline Bynum, Stevan Harrell, and Paula Richman, eds., *Gender and Religion: On the Complexity of Symbols* (Boston: Beacon Press, 1986), 13.

6. Arthur W. Shippee, "Islam and the History of Religions," in *Humanities Magazine* (May/June 1990):30.

7. Harry Slochower, *Mythopoesis* (Detroit: Wayne State University Press, 1970), 47-66.

8. D. Capps and F. Reynolds, *The Biographical Process* (The Hague: Mouton, 1976), 1-30.

9. Anne C. Klein, "Primordial Purity and Everyday Life: Exalted Female Symbols and the Women of Tibet," in Clarissa W. Atkinson, Constance H. Buchanan, and Margaret R. Miles, eds., *Immaculate and Powerful* (Boston: Beacon Press, 1985), 111-138.

10. A.R. Gibb, "Islamic Biographical Literature," in B. Lewis and Holt, eds., *Historians of the Middle East* (London: Oxford, 1962), 54.

11. The nickname "al-ḥumayra" refers to the coloring of 'Ā'isha's fair skin made radiant by a light sunburn (see Fatima Mernissi, *Women and Islam* [Oxford: Blackwell, 1991], 78).

12. Kaukab Siddique, *Liberation of Women Thru Islam* (Kingsville, MD: American Society for Education and Religion, 1990), 32-33.

13. Fāṭima, 'Alī, and the twelve Imams who are their descendants.

14. According to a saying of the Prophet they are 'Āṣiyya, wife of Pharaoh, Mary, Khadīja, and Fāṭima.

15. Jane MacAuliffe, "Chosen of All Women: Mary and Fāṭima in Quranic Exegesis," *Islamochristiana* 7 (1981):19-28.

16. 'Alī Sharī'atī, *Fāṭima is Fāṭima*, trans. Laleh Bakhtiyar, (Tehran: Shariati Foundation, 1980).

17. Zainab, daughter of Fāṭima and 'Alī, is a heroine in her own right who "continues the movement at a time when all of the heroes of the revolution are dead and the breath of the forerunners of Islam has ceased in the midst of our people..." (Sharī'atī, 43).

18. Sharī'atī, 165. See also Marcia Hermansen, "Fāṭima as a Role Model for the Iranian Woman of Today in the Works of 'Alī Sharī'atī," in Guity Nashat, ed., *Women and Revolution in Iran* (Boulder, CO: Westview Press, 1983), 87-96.

19. Alia Schleiffer, *Motherhood in Islam* (Cambridge, UK: Islamic Academy, 1986), 54. This honoring of the mother who dies in childbirth is not unique to the Islamic tradition. In ancient Sparta women who died in childbirth and male warriors were specially memorialized on tombstones. This is perhaps due to the fact that these two types in particular embodied dominant cultural values.

20. Ibn Sa'd, *Kitāb al-Ṭabaqāt al-Kabīr* VIII (Leiden: E.J. Brill, 1905-1940), 304.

21. Ibn Sa'd, VIII, 193.

22. Ibn Sa'd, VIII, 27, 29.

23. Syed Sulaimān Nadvī, *Heroic Deeds of Muslim Women*, trans. Syed Sabāhuddīn Abdur Rahmān, (New Delhi: International Islamic Publishers, 1985), 23.

24. Nadvī, 26-27.

25. Nadvī, 28.

26. Muhammad Zakariyya Kaandhlawī, *Stories of the Sahaabah* (Johannesburg: Waterval Islamic Institute, 1987), 180-182.

27. See for example Marfisa in the Charlemagne/Roland cycle, Nicolette in *Aucassin et Nicollette*, and Guiborc in the William cycle.

28. Marina Warner, *Joan of Arc: The Image of Female Heroism* (New York: Vintage Books, 1982).

29. Firdausī, *The Epic of the Kings*, trans. Reuben Levy (London: Routledge and Kegan Paul, 1967). This work, which celebrates mainly pre-Islamic Persian heroes, contains stories about a number of the champions who are bested or at least challenged by heroic foreign women. Marriage to foreign princesses is a common motif. Examples of these heroines are Rudāba, mother of the champion Rustam, and Gordāfarīd, a woman warrior. A work presenting the heroines of Persian epics in English is Bapsy Pavry, *The Heroines of Ancient Persia, Stories Retold from the Shāhnāmeh of Ferdowsī* (Cambridge: Cambridge University Press, 1930).

30. This is a series of Arabic folk poetic romances told by popular story tellers in North Africa and other Arab regions (*La Geste Hilalienne version de Bou Thadi* [Tunisie]; trans. Lucienne Saada [Paris: Gallimard, 1985]). This cycle has been studied by Bridgette Connelly, *Arabic Folk Epic* (Berkeley: University of California, 1986). The main heroine is called Jāziyya (or Zāziyya). See also M. Galley, "Femmes de la Geste Hilalienne," *Litterature Orale Arabo-Berbere* 15 (1984): 31-44. Other Arab folk heroines are Fātima Bint Birrī (Egypt) (see Hasan M. El-Shamy, "The Story of el-Sayyid Ahmad al-Badawī with Fātima Bint Birrī: An Introduction," *Folklore Forum* 10, No. 1 [1977]: 1-13), and 'Abla in the 'Antar cycle).

31. I am indebted to an unpublished paper by John Renard for this summary of the conclusions of R. Grech, "Le Recit heroique de source arabe," *Libyca* 25 (1977): 319-328. Renard has recently completed a monograph on the hero motif in Islamic civilization (forthcoming from University of South Carolina Press).

32. Sandra Danforth, "The Social and Political Implications of Muslim Middle Eastern Women's Participation in Violent Political Conflict," *Women and Politics* 4, No. 1 (Spring 1984): 35-53.

33. Mariam Cooke, *War's Other Voices: Women Writers of the Lebanese Civil War* (Cambridge: Cambridge University Press, 1987).

34. Ṭabarī, *Mohammed, Sceau des prophetes*, trans. Hermann Zotenberg (Paris: Sindbad, 1980), 286; quoted in Mernissi, 117.

35. Mernissi, 286.

36. Ibn Ishāq, *The Life of Muhammad*, trans. A. Guillaume (Karachi: Oxford University Press, 1980), 359.

37. Jan Knappert, *Islamic Legends* 1, *Nisāba* 15 #1 (Leiden: E.J. Brill, 1985), 403-404. Although Knappert is not specific about the source of this tale, the character names and details of the story suggest that it is a variant of the Indo-Persian Dastān-e-Amīr Ḥamza cycle studied by Frances W. Pritchett in *The Romance Tradition in Urdu* (New York: Columbia University Press, 1991).

38. Mernissi, 192-193.

39. Margaret Smith, *Rābi'a and Her Fellow Mystics in Islam* (London: Oxford, 1926).

40. Javād Nūrbakhsh, *Sufi Women* (London: Khānqāhī Ni'matullāhī Publications, 1990), 17.

41. Pearson and Pope, 3.

42. Nūrbakhsh, 18.

43. Nūrbakhsh, 26-28; Smith, 75.

44. Pearson and Pope, 14.

45. Quoted in Nūrbakhsh, 28.

46. Nūrbakhsh, 27.

47. Nūrbakhsh, 25.

48. Nūrbakhsh, 24.

49. Nūrbakhsh, 27.

50. Nūrbakhsh, 15.

51. Jāmī, *Nafahāt al-Uns*, ed. Mahdī Tauhīdipūr (Tehran: Kitābfurūshī Mahmūdī, 1337 Shamsī, 1969), 615. In Arabic, a grammatically gendered language, the main word for Sun (shams) is feminine and that for Moon is masculine.

52. Farīduddīn 'Attār, *Muslim Saints and Mystics*, trans. A.J. Arberry (Chicago: University of Chicago, 1966), 40.

53. 'Alī Sharī'atī, *Hajj*, trans. 'Alī A. Behzādnia and Najla Denny (Houston: Free Islamic Literatures, 1974).

54. Sharī'atī, *Hajj*, 39.

55. Sharī'atī, *Hajj*, 39-40. The last sentence refers to the belief that Hagar is the only person accorded the honor of being buried in the Ka'ba.

56. Sharī'atī, *Hajj*, 40.

57. Sharī'atī, *Hajj*, 41-45. This resonates with a recent attempt to recover the significance of Hagar in the Biblical tradition.

"There is no question that Hagar must be redeemed for Muslim as well as Jewish and Christian women. Her courage in the face of adversity, her faith in herself and in her destiny, guided by her own spiritual power, must be a revelation to all women. Above all, her close relationship with divinity and her inspiration to forge her own community must not be forgotten" (Savina J. Teubal, *Hagar the Egyptian* [San Francisco: Harper and Row, 1990], 200).

58. Qur'ān 12:31.

59. A folk version of the story is summarized in Knappert, 104. A well-known literary version of the story is Jāmī, *Yūsuf va Zulaykha* (Irvine: Intishārāt-i-Irānzamīn, 1983); for an English translation see Jami, *Yusuf and Zulaikha by 'Abdul Rahmān Jāmī*, trans. David Pendlebury (London: Octagon Press, 1980).

60. This refers to a hadith report of the Prophet, "My community will not agree on an error," which carries a normative force in establishing consensus as a principle of Islamic law.

61. Ira Lapidus, "Adulthood in Islam: Religious Maturity in the Islamic Tradition," *Daedalus* 105 (1976): 93-107.

62. Joseph Campbell, *The Hero with A Thousand Faces* (New York: Pantheon Books, 1949), 337; quoted in Pearson and Pope, 9.

63. Michael C. Hillmann, *Iranian Culture: A Persianist View* (Lanham, MD: University Press of America, 1990), 30-41. The story of Rustam and Sohrāb occurs in Firdausī's epic *Shāhnāmeh*.

64. Mernissi, *Women and Islam*; Siddique, *Liberation of Women Thru Islam*; Nadvī, *Heroic Deeds of Muslim*

Women; Barbara Daly Metcalf, *Perfecting Women: Maulānā Ashraf 'Alī Thanawī's Bihishtī Zēwar* (Berkeley: University of California Press, 1990).

65. Bint al-Shāṭī, *Umm al-Nabī*, (Cairo: Dār al-Hilāl, 1961); *Baṭalāt Karbalā* (Cairo: 1965); *Nisā al-Nabī* (Cairo: Dar al-Hilal, 1961); *Sukayna bint al-Ḥusain* (Cairo: 1965). See also Issa J. Boullata, "A Study of Bint al-Shāṭi's Method (of exegesis)," *Muslim World* 64, No. 2 (April 1974): 102-103; C. Kooij, "Bint al-Shāṭi': A Suitable Case for Biography," in *The Challenge of the Middle East*, eds., Ibrahim el-Sheikh, C. Aart van de Koppel and Rudolph Peters (Amsterdam: University of Amsterdam, Institute for Modern Near Eastern Studies, 1982).

66. Mernissi, *Women and Islam*. For a brief survey of contemporary thought and literature by Arab women, see Issa J. Boullata, "Voices of Arab Women," in *Trends and Issues in Contemporary Arab Thought* (Albany, N.Y.: State University of New York Press, 1990), 119-137.

67. Miriam Cooke, paper presented at the American Academy of Religion, Nov. 1991. On Zainab al-Ghazzālī, see Valerie Hoffman, "An Islamic Activist: Zaynab al-Ghazzālī," in Elizabeth Fernea, ed., *Women and the Family in the Middle East* (Austin, TX: University of Texas Press, 1985), 233-254.

68. Miriam Cooke, *War's Other Voices;* Laila Ahmed, "Arab Culture and Writing Women's Bodies," *Feminist Issues* 9, No. 1 (1989): 41-55.

FLORENCE NIGHTINGALE : A STUDY IN HEROIC ALTRUISM

Sheila McDonough

The wounded from the battle-plain,
In dreary hospitals of pain,
The cheerless corridors,
The cold and stony floors.

Lo! in that house of misery
A lady with a lamp I see
Pass through the glimmering gloom,
And flit from room to room....

A Lady with a Lamp shall stand
In the great history of the land
A noble type of good
Heroic womanhood.[1]

This widely read poem of the late-nineteenth century helped create a public image of the lady with the lamp. This particular vision of the role and accomplishments of Florence Nightingale became the unofficial stereotype of her "good heroic womanhood." Although the British Cabinet had explicitly given her the title, "superintendent of the female nursing establishment," nevertheless the word "flit" in this poem tends to obscure her management role and emphasizes a service rather than an authoritative function. The poem shows her as a hero, but as a type of hero who conformed to the public stereotype of the merciful, serving female. The acknowledgment of heroic service was made, but it was conveyed through an image of lightweight, angelic, butterfly-like flitting. This portrayal allowed the public to continue thinking of the feminine as delicate, gentle, and quite different from the heavy moral seriousness of the masculine. Masculine qualities were presumed to be superior and necessary for males who were believed to be the divinely appointed protectors of the lightweight butterflies.

At this time in the mid-nineteenth century, when the Crimean War pitted the British, French and Turkish armies against the Russians in a series of battles along the shores of the Black Sea, the law in England still denied any control over property to married women. The husband's authority over all aspects of a family's life was strongly enforced through legal and religious structures. Women were not supposed to take part in political or public life; they were certainly not to vote and not to work outside the home except perhaps as governesses. For the British Cabinet to send a woman of good family off to work for them in Turkey was an act contrary to public notions of decency and propriety. She was sent, moreover, not to flit but to superintend, which, in fact, meant to bring some order out of the chaos in the military hospitals caused by inefficient bureaucracy and inept military and medical officials. She required the title of superintendent because she had to exercise authority over her small group of nurses.

Miss Nightingale reported regularly not only to the Cabinet but also to Queen Victoria. When the Queen and the Prince Consort met Miss Nightingale after the War and after her considerable success in transforming the nature of British military hospitals, Prince Albert recorded the event in his diary as follows: "She put before us all the defects of our present military hospital system and the reforms that are needed. We are much pleased with her." The Queen wrote to the Commander-in-Chief: "I wish we had her at the War Office."[2] The Queen also said that this woman could probably run the military services better than the generals and admirals; this is no small compliment to the administrative abilities of Miss Nightingale. The royal statement, coming from one who read reports and analysed problems herself, indicates that the Queen recognised the intellectual power of the Nursing Superintendent who was telling her very clearly why wounded men died in such large numbers. Miss Nightingale sent reports buttressed with precise details concerning the loss of lives due to incompetence. The Queen discerned a good intellect in someone who was ahead of her time. The general public, however, could respond to female heroism only in the form of the flitting butterfly.

Why was the image of a flitting lady with a lamp the female hero most acceptable to the mid-nineteenth century British public? If a woman were to be acknowledged (1) as a more competent administrator than the male doctors and military men who were running the military hospitals, and (2) as a powerful reformer of corrupt public bureaucracies, then the whole social system of patriarchal control of women might be threatened. There was a belief, supported allegedly by revelation and reason, that women must be protected and controlled by men. To challenge this belief with the concrete example of a woman's independence and heroic actions might destabilize society. So the heroine could be affirmed but only in images that would not allow the real force of her character and intellect to be recognised. Would she have been surprised by this? Probably not in the least.

The Heroic Altruism of a Nurse

Miss Nightingale understood the prejudices of her society and was simply not prepared to subscribe to, or be dominated by, them. She said God had called her when she was sixteen. Although she did not know for many years what form her vocation might take, she was sufficiently influenced by this conviction about her calling that she adamantly refused all acceptable social roles. For ten years, she was harassed by family for her non-conformity. After a difficult struggle, she refused marriage to an attractive, wealthy man whom she nevertheless continued to regard as a good friend. Her decision not to marry was not a refusal of the particular man, but a refusal of the limitations created by the role of wife in her society. She would not restrict herself to the activities permitted to good wives. To the fury of her mother and sister, she (a wealthy and attractive woman) refused all the social benefits of her position in society, insisting instead on entering dirty hospitals where nursing was usually linked with drunkenness, prostitution, disorder, and disease.

To educate herself about hospital life, she spent some time working at Kaiserswerth, Germany, in a new training school established by a Lutheran pastor. She also spent time in Rome and Paris in Roman Catholic convents and hospitals. She was attracted by the ideal of service but was not prepared to accept Roman Catholic discipline. The Roman Catholic Cardinal Manning knew and admired her but commented that Roman Catholicism would not do for her because she would never obey.[3] She alone would interpret her calling.

A glimpse of her convictions can be seen in a piece of fiction entitled *Cassandra*, which she wrote two years before her departure to the Crimea. Cassandra was the name of the Trojan princess cursed by her possession of accurate knowledge of the future that none would believe. Florence Nightingale had acquired a good knowledge of Greek and Latin from her study at home. That she chose such a name for her character tells us something about her perceptions of her own life. The manuscript was not published at the time, but a number of copies were circulated privately. The pages describe the life of a young girl who must constantly suppress herself to do what others want. She must spend her days reading aloud to members of her family, arranging flowers, and serving tea; she must never pursue any activity seriously for a length of time; she must continually make polite conversation. Finally, Cassandra dies, as if "killed" by her family. Florence Nightingale put the following words in her young heroine's mouth:

> My people were like children, ... I was their hobby horse, their plaything; and they drove me to and fro, dear souls! never weary of the play themselves, till I, who had grown to woman's estate, and to the ideas of the nineteenth century, lay down exhausted, my mind closed to hope, my heart to strength, ... Welcome beautiful death.[4]

These pages give considerable insight into the thinking of the young woman who would, two years later at the age of thirty-four, accept the challenge of bringing order into the chaotic military hospitals in the Crimea. In her writing, she contrasted with some bitterness the current social ideal of womanhood — having no passion, no serious purpose, and no steadiness of will — with her own ideal of passion, dedication and strength of will. The offer to go to the Crimea seemed a heaven-sent chance to escape from an infantilising role and become involved in real, adult responsibilities. It was an opportunity made available to very few women of her class.

What was the work like in the Crimean hospitals? A journal written by one of the young nurses who went with the new superintendent to the British hospitals in Turkey provides some clues. Sarah Anne Terrot, an Anglican nun, described the instructions given by the Secretary of War and Miss Nightingale as the nurses prepared to leave England:

> We received our papers of agreement, and with the other nurses received instructions from Mr. Sidney Herbert. He spoke of our duties — of modesty and propriety, of enduring hardness, and of carefully avoiding religious proselytizing; and

ended by thanking us for being willing to engage
in an office which might be a very great comfort to
the poor men who had suffered for their country
.... There we met Miss Nightingale, and from the
first moment I felt an impulse to love, trust, and
respect her. Her appearance and manner impressed
me with a sense of goodness and wisdom, of high
mental powers highly cultivated and devoted to
highest ends.[5]

After a difficult journey by sea to Turkey, the nurses found
themselves in the hospital at Scutari. Nurse Sarah Anne recorded
in her journal the following comments:

These wards were at this time very unfit for use.
The roof let in water; the windows were rickety,
and were sometimes blown in on dying men; the
broken windows were stuffed with rags — everything looked deplorable and depressing.... One
poor dying fellow, called Nicols, seemed to be
neglected by the orderlies because he was dying.
He was very dirty, covered with wounds, and
devoured by lice. I pointed this out to the orderlies, whose only excuse was — "It's not worth
while to clean him; he's not long for this world."
I washed his face and hands, cut away his hair,
and tried to make him a little less uncomfort-
able.... His flannel shirt was dark, and seemed
moving with lice, it stuck into his bed-sores....
Daily we saw men carried in whose state of filth
no words can describe, and with death written on
their discoloured faces ... we were generally sent
to the few cases of cholera.... Most of them were
fatal.... This was in a small ward containing eight
or ten beds, and during the next day all the patients

in it except two died.... Miss Nightingale afterwards went with Mr. Maclean into the deadhouse,
where above ten who had died that day lay. It was
an awful place to visit at any time, and as I waited
at the door and saw her calmly uncover the faces
of the dead, and look on them as they lay far from
wife or mother in that dreary place, it seemed
strange to see one so frail, graceful, and refined
standing at the dead of night alone amid such sad
scenes of mortality.[6]

These brief glimpses provide some insight into the conditions
facing the nurses. There were open drains from the wards filled
with human and animal excrement. The water supply contained
a dead horse. Miss Nightingale dealt quickly, practically, and
energetically with many such problems that had previously been
left unattended because of inertia, fatalism, and inefficiency.

Her virtues included tact and political savoir faire.
Although she met opposition from doctors and bureaucrats, she
also made many allies. During the few years she was in Turkish
hospitals, great changes took place. In 1855, 11,325 men out of
an army of 30,000 were admitted to hospital. Of these, 3,168
died. On average, 36 per cent died before Miss Nightingale and
the nurses came. The next year it was only 5.2 per cent.[7] One
commentator noted,

the change that Florence Nightingale brought
about is strikingly illuminated by comparing the
figures for deaths from disease, ... in 1854 and
1856. In 1854 [before she arrived] there were
2,373 British who died and 1,857 French. In
1856 [after her work] the figures were 17,129
French [an alarming number that was in part
accounted for by a severe epidemic of typhus — a
louse-borne disease that typically occurs in over-

crowded, unhygienic conditions] and only 218 British.

During her years of uncertainty, Florence Nightingale had acquired a detailed understanding of the principles of sanitation and it was the inspired way she succeeded in having these applied in the hospitals ... that made the transformation possible. No amount of determination, or of political influence, or of public outrage on their own could have achieved these results. Nor indeed could the presence of female nurses, as evidenced by the misfortunes of the French and Russians. Florence Nightingale went to Scutari as an administrator; to achieve her purpose she had to have nurses who would obey her will. Sarah Anne and the others in that original small party were the essential instruments of her genius."[8]

Because she was good in mathematics, she became a practical innovator in the use of statistics in hospital administration (e.g., the relevant factors relating to the number of wounded, number of beds, and number of dying). It is the clarity of her mental powers in organising and recording this data by herself that so impressed the Queen and others. She always backed up her arguments with detailed statistics. She also could argue her case well, winning most of her bureaucratic battles.

A deeper accomplishment lay in changing attitudes towards sick persons. Robert Richardson, an historian of medicine, has commented that before Miss Nightingale's work in the Crimea, it was not uncommon to find among the military leaders an attitude that the wounded were no longer important because they could not play a role in the absorbing game of war.[9] The terrible hospital conditions were partly attributable to this common view. Miss Nightingale and her small band of nurses changed these priorities in a radical way. She was unwilling to accept male authority as absolute and usually managed to get her way by diplomatically manipulating the various authority structures. She was a reformer, however, not a revolutionary.

When she returned to England, Miss Nightingale continued to exercise her influence on behalf of many causes. The most important of these was the Nightingale School for Nurses. Money was raised by public subscription for the establishment of the training school for nurses. Fifteen candidates were accepted for the first class; it was understood that they were to be educated to train others. It was also understood that the many opponents of this radical innovation would be looking for evidence of incompetence or immorality among these Nightingale disciples. For this and other reasons, they were selected and trained with great care and attention to every detail of their lives. Every month a moral and technical records were prepared for each of them. Each student had to keep a personal diary, which Miss Nightingale herself read every month. She wanted to be sure of the quality of every one of the graduates because she was aware of the need to protect the new experiment from the criticism of its opponents.[10] As we noted above, the system worked; the graduates went forth, trained others in their turn, and translated their mentor's vision concretely into institutional patterns of life and work.

In 1859 she wrote a popular little book entitled *Notes on Nursing*.[11] 15,000 copies of the book were sold within a month of its first publication, and it has been reprinted many times since. It was translated into French, German and Italian; thousands of copies were distributed in factories, villages and schools. Among its virtues, the book had much to say about the relationship of hygiene to health. One of her biographers comments that "neither its good sense nor its wit has dated,"[12] and that it can still be read with enjoyment. There is no doubt that she knew exactly what she wanted done with respect to the training of nurses. A great many of the graduates became heads of institutions and educators of further generations.

Miss Nightingale's personal vision and discipline were comparable to that of some medieval mystics who founded religious orders. Just as St. Francis, for example, left behind him an order of persons committed to relating to the world in the pattern devised by him, so also Miss Nightingale devised a system through which other women might learn to achieve some of the habits of thought and work that she had brought into being. The nursing profession developed in considerable measure along the guidelines set down by her.

The Religious Foundations of Miss Nightingale's Heroic Altruism

There is much that we will never know about Miss Nightingale personal religious disciplines and her feelings about the sufferings she encountered. It is clear, however, that she had worked out her basic religious attitudes in the years before she went to the Crimea. The letters written in 1848 when she visited Italy with her friends reflect her responsiveness to the beauty of Italian churches, painting and sculpture. She commented that Catholics understand the cultivation of the imagination better than anyone.[13] She was deeply moved by a visit to St. Peter's by moonlight. She knew that her family might find her enthusiastic writings about the beauties of Roman Catholic life and art troubling if it indicated a tendency to conversion, but she assured them in several ways that such a conclusion was unlikely. Commenting on how much her father's teaching had meant to her, she said:

> I assure you, I feel more and more every day my
> gratitude to that father, who taught me all I ever
> knew, who gave me all the ideas I ever had, who
> taught me interest in nations as though they were
> personal existences, and showed me how to look

upon all churches as but parts of the one great
scheme, all opinions, political and religious, as but
as accidental developments of the one Parent Sap
which comes up oats in one case and oranges in
another.[14]

Throughout her life, Miss Nightingale retained the
conviction that all traditions contain some truth, and that no one
tradition contains everything. With respect to the competing
claims of Protestants and Catholics she wrote,

> Today [New Year's Eve] I set off before breakfast
> to St. Peter's to refresh and to spend the last
> morning of the old year in the company of all the
> prophets, patriarchs and archangels ... in those
> colossal mosaics.... I should have been disap-
> pointed in the Vespers at the Gesu this afternoon
> ... if it had not been that it does one so much good
> to lay aside for a moment, one's own individual
> sin and misery and join the great worship of
> heaven and earth — the four organs at the Gesu
> seeming to bring in the sound from the four
> winds.... The Pope looked beautiful, as he always
> does, without any physical beauty at all — and his
> Blessing did one good.... Are you afraid that I am
> becoming a Roman Catholic? I might perhaps , if
> there had been anything in me for Roman
> Catholicism to lay hold of, but I was not a Protes-
> tant before. Protestantism is confining Inspiration
> to one period, one nation, and one place, if I
> understand it right, and within that period, that
> nation, and that place of inspiration, allowing you
> all possible freedom of interpretation and thought.
> Catholicism allows Inspiration to all times, all
> nations, and all place ... but limits the inspiration

of God to herself as its only channel. Can either
of these be true? Can the 'word' be pinned down?
All churches are, of course, only more of less
unsuccessful attempts to represent the unseen to
the mind, to give form to 'things hoped for,'
intangible. A church rises because it has succeeded in doing this for a certain class of minds, at
a certain period. It falls when another mind, or
another period, requires another and different
representation to give life to its unseen. When the
day shall come when our ... ideas require *no* form,
then people will cease to use the word 'My *church*
when they mean 'My *religion*' and will not con-
fuse, as now, 'My theology' with 'My *faith*' any
more than they imagine 'My *native language*' to
be 'My*self*' or 'My *mind*'. As the language is to
the mind, expressing and by reaction influencing
it, so is theology to faith, but God forbid, that we
should really degrade faith to be nothing more
than a language![15]

In another letter she explains why, in spite of her attraction to
Catholicism, she would not convert.

Believing, as I really do, that the Catholic Church
is the least unsuccessful attempt, which any church
has made, to represent the Unseen in tangible
form, I never could nevertheless become a Catholic, because ... the very principle, which makes
me admire and love Catholicism, is that which
would cease, or would never have had existence,
if I were a Catholic. Ah dear soul, I have known
too well the want of Liberty in word and action,
ever to forfeit that of thought. And by liberty I do
not mean insubordination ... I mean the power of

perceiving truly, that is feeling (according to the
measure of one's capacity) as the Creator may be
supposed to feel about such or such object, which
is truth (Liberty is only truth in action) and having
perceived truly, to will rightly, that is, in accord-
ance to His will, and then, unfettered by factitious
circumstances, unwarped by accessory consideration, to do what you have willed (where it be in
the Subjective or Objective kingdom, that is, in
yourself or in the external world), to speak what
you have thought — this will be always, of course,
in obedience to the laws of God, for in this way
you become yourself a law of God.[16]

These words, written six years before she went to the Crimea,
show us how her faith inspired her efforts to make the law of God
visible to her fellow creatures. She was convinced that once
people had a clear insight into ultimate truth, then they should
exercise the will to model themselves on that truth and to change
the world. In her case, truth involved a conviction that human life
could be better, more merciful and just. Human effort was
required to overturn unjust and oppressive systems.

Her religious perspective included the idea that divine
inspiration is not limited to any time, place or person because all
human efforts to express the intangible are inadequate. Hence,
the more a person was unfettered and open, the more a person
might discern ways to express the ineffable. Thus, in Rome she
could find great beauty in Christian Churches but also in the
Pantheon, a remnant of the religion of ancient Rome.

She also thought the capacities for spiritual awareness of
women differed from those of men. In her comments on the
paintings in the Sistine chapel, she writes,

The difference between the characters of man and
woman is so extraordinarily kept.... The Padre

Eterno having breathed into Adam the breath of
life, is just leaving him, committing to him his last
behests.... There is however, nothing of the
inward consciousness of the Divine Presence in it;
no speaking purely from *heart* to *heart* — the
Creator had made himself known to man by an
outward manifestation, and man has understood
and accepted it ... but any body looking at the
Creation of *Woman*, will see the difference —
there she kneels, the lovely new born woman,
before her Creator, who, in his unspeakable Goodness, has stripped himself of all his Power and his
Majesty, and stands before her in the semblance of
a man, her father, and her friend, and yet, such is
the sublime idea of M. Angelo, that there is
nothing lost of dignity in the figure. Adam continues sleeping. No woman would have done this,
she should have been warned (by her quicker
perception) of the presence of a supernatural
being. Eve, kneeling in perfect love and devotion,
receives with entire submission, the commands of
her Creator, which come straight from His *spirit*
to hers, without any material manifestation of
Power. She is lovely beyond description.[17]

Miss Nightingale conceived of her obedience to her
vocation in a way similar to Eve's obedience to God. She knew,
of course, that the Fall was the next chapter of the story of
creation, and she describes Michelangelo's depiction of that event
with similarly vivid appreciation.

Adam regrets, departs, and it is done. Eve,
crouching and heart stricken, scarcely giving a
thought to what she has lost, nor to the material
punishment awarded her, is an image of the

anguish of the soul, the long inward writhings of
remorse, which receive no alleviation ... from
eternal things. She seems literally 'swallowed up'
by self-abasement. This is a wonderful conception.[18]

Reading in Michelangelo's painting an ideal of the spiritual power
of the feminine vocation, Miss Nightingal had a sense of the
female as more alert to divine presence and more ready to
undergo the anguish of spiritual alienation than the more forth-
right and obtuse male. Her culture was one that assumed essential
differences in male and female natures. She does not appear to
have questioned that assumption. Yet she uses it, as indicated in
her notion of Eve, to suggest a greater spiritual and human
vocation for women precisely because they, more sensitive to
spiritual reality and more aware of the radical alienation between
the divine and the human, ought to be quicker to respond to
spiritual imperatives. Most people of her time used the notion of
the more spiritual female to justify keeping women in the home
and uncorrupted by the male world; Miss Nightingale uses the
same notion for urging women to work in society and to reform
the evils in the world.

Her lack of belief in male judgment applied also to
religious authorities. She would not accept either the authority of
the Roman Catholic Church or of the Bible. When asked in later
life to give her views on how to teach children the Bible, she
wrote,

The story of Achilles and his horses is far more fit
for children than that of Balaam and his ass, which
is only fit to be told to asses. The stories of
Samson and of Jepthah are only fit to be told to
bull dogs; and the story of Bathsheba to be told to
Bathshebas. Yet we give all these stories to
children as 'Holy Writ.' There are some things in

Homer we might better call 'Holy Writ' — many, many in Sophocles and Aeschylus. The stories about Andromache and Antigone are worth all the women in the Old Testament put together, nay, almost all the women in the Bible.[19]

Some of the portraits we have of her show her with her favorite pet, an owl named Athena, at her side. The goddess Athena was known as owl-eyed. If we put this affection for Athena together with her remarks about Andromache and Antigone, we see that Miss Nightingale had acquired from her readings in Greek literature ideas different from those of her family and society. She perceived in the ideal of Athena as the wise governor of the city, and in the struggles of heroic women in Greek drama, an awareness of female capacities for courage, self-reliance, and effective action different from anything taught in Christian Sunday Schools. The unmarried Athena is the archetypical example of female wisdom independent of any reliance on, or support from males: Athena, standing tall above her city, governs wisely, supports arts and crafts, maintains justice and good order. Her wisdom is the source of the peaceful well-being of the people. When her warriors must fight, she guides and sustains them. Many male thinkers in the nineteenth century (for example, Matthew Arnold and Friedrich Nietzsche) were finding new inspiration in Greek thought leading them away from an exclusive reliance on the Bible as a source of insight. Miss Nightingale was one of several women who recognised that Greek myth and drama could reawaken women's awareness of capacities in themselves that many had for centuries been refusing to acknowledge or respect.

During the early 1850s when she spent time in Roman Catholic institutions and was thinking about religious commitment, she also spent time investigating attitudes toward religion among the working classes. She discovered a general disenchantment with all churches. In response, she became interested in the idea that free thought is not incompatible with belief in God. She described God as the "spirit of truth" and affirmed that moral laws are fixed.[20] Ultimately, she sided neither with the anti-clerical revolutionaries nor the church. In Jowett's correspondence with her, he suggested that she write something on what she understood as the "character of God," since that was a phrase she often used. In response she wrote three essays on the laws of the moral world, two of which were published in *Fraser's Magazine* in 1873. One title was "A Sub-Note of Interrogation: What will our Religion be in 1991"[21] Such a title suggests that she thought of herself as a hundred years ahead of her time. From the perspective of 1992, we can be sure she would be pleased with the changes that have occurred with respect to the laws relating to women's property, the right to work and vote, and the ordination of women. And, of course, our clean and efficient hospitals are a living tribute to her. However, on religious matters, it is doubtful she would think a hundred years had caused much positive and effective change.

In later life, she hoped to publish a volume of writings by medieval Christian mystics. Although this did not happen, her intention indicates an acquaintance with such writings. It seems probable that she used them throughout her troubled life as a source of encouragement and direction. When considering religious experience, we normally acknowledge that we cannot comprehend the ineffable quality of the experience itself, but we can consider how the experience transforms people and their activities. I would maintain that Florence Nightingale was a mystic in the classical sense of a person single-mindedly absorbed by her own particular vision. She held to that vision in the face of various obstacles.

She regularly read writings by mystics regardless of their tradition (e.g., St. John of the Cross and St. Theresa). While serving in the Crimea, she worked with a Roman Catholic nun, Rev. Mother Bermondsey; the two read together medieval mystics such as Mother Julian of Norwich. In her later correspondence with Jowett, she commented on the similarities between the medieval mystics and Plato. She referred in particular to the prayer in Plato's *Phaedrus*: "give me beauty in the inward soul and may the inward and outward man be at one." These few words encompassed, she thought, almost all of St. John of the Cross.[22] She also wrote,

> The "mystical" state is the essence of common sense ... the ecstatic sense is unreal, and should not be at all ... we can only act and speak and think through Him; and what we need is to discover such laws of His as will enable us to be always acting and thinking in conscious concert with Him.... There will be no Heaven unless we make it.... Desire for personal salvation is not religion.[23]

The idea of God in her thought seems to indicate the possibility of perfection. God's work in the world was to be directed towards greater perfection of all persons and human institutions. Her acceptance of the challenge to go to the Crimea was an expression of her conviction that human energies should be directed towards transforming the conditions of misery and suffering in the world. Even those who held to the simplistic lady of the lamp picture knew that something strange and unusually moving was occurring as she moved among the discarded victims of war. Most of them probably did not realise that she was effectively transforming certain institutions of her social world. From her perspective, such transformation would be part of the movement towards greater perfection for all human life. To move towards greater perfection would be to discover the underlying harmony that ought to exist between the absolute and the human realms.

Notes

1. Henry Wadsworth Longfellow, "Saint Filamena," *Atlantic Monthly* 1 (1857): 22-23; cited in Elizabeth K. Helsinger, et. al, *The Woman Question: Society and Literature in Britain and America, 1837-1883* (New York, Garland Publishing, 1983), 143.

2. Cecil Woodham-Smith, *Florence Nightingale, 1820-1910* (London: Constable, 1951), 265.

3. Woodham-Smith, 100.

4. Woodham-Smith, 95.

5. Robert Richardson, ed., *Nurse Sarah Anne With Florence Nightingale at Scutari* (London: John Murray, 1977), 66.

6. Richardson, 87-99.

7. Richardson, 48.

8. Richardson, 50, 51.

9. Richardson, 35, 36.

10. Woodham-Smith, 346-348.

11. Florence Nightingale, *Notes on Nursing* (London: Churchill Livingstone, 1980), 6.

12. Mary Raymond Andrews, *A Lost Commander: Florence Nightingale* (New York: Doubleday, 1933), 183; Woodham-Smith, 338.

13. Mary Keele, ed., *Florence Nightingale in Rome: Letters Written by Florence Nightingale in Rome in the Winter of 1847-1848* (Philadelphia: American Philosophical Society, 1981), 206.

14. Keele, 146.

15. Keele, 154, 155.

16. Keele, 220.

17. Keele, 171.

18. Keele, 172.

19. Woodham-Smith, 523.

20. Woodham-Smith, 99, 100.

21. Woodham-Smith, 522.

22. Woodham-Smith, 524, 525.

23. Woodham-Smith, 525.

Contributors

Kathryn Hansen
Professor
Department of Asian Studies
1871 West Mall
University of British Columbia
Vancouver, B.C.
V6T 1Z2

Fan Pen Chen
Assistant Professor
East Asian Language & Literatures
400-C Arts
University of Alberta
Edmonton, AB
T6G 2H4

Sheila McDonough
Professor
Department of Religion
Concordia University
2060 Mackay Ave.
Montreal, PQ
H3G 1M8

Nalini Devdas
Associate Professor
Department of Religion
Rm. 2121, Dunton Tower
Carleton University
Ottawa, ON
K1S 5B6

Marcia K. Hermansen
Associate Professor
Religious Studies
San Diego State University
San Diego, CA
92182

On Manuscript Submission

The editors of *Women in World Religions* welcome articles, books for review, book reviews, and suggestions. Major articles should be between 30 and 40 typed, double-spaced pages (5000 to 7530 words) in length, including notes, appendices, and bibliography. Style should conform to the following Notes for Electronic Text Preparation. For additional details see *The Chicago Manual of Style*. The conventions of American spelling should be followed. An abstract of no more than 500 words should accompany the article, and a brief *curriculum vitae* of the author should be enclosed.

Submissions should be addressed to:

The Editors
Women in World Religions
Faculty of Religious Studies
McGill University
3520 University Street
Montreal, Quebec
Canada H3A 2A7

Notes for Electronic Text Preparation

General

The word-processed text should be in single column format. Keep the layout of the text as simple as possible; in particular, do not use the word-processor's options to justify the text or to hyphenate the words.

The final text should be submitted both in manuscript form and on diskette. Use standard 3 1/2" or 5 1/4" diskettes for this purpose.

Both double density (DD) and high density (HD) diskettes are acceptable. Make sure, however, that the diskettes are formatted according to their capacity (HD or DD) before copying the files onto them. The format of the files depends on the wordprocessor used. Texts made with WordPerfect (4.2 or higher) or ASCII format can be readily processed.

It is essential that the name and version of the wordprocessing program and the type of computer on which the text was prepared be clearly indicated on the diskette label.

References

For references follow the latest edition of *The Chicago Manual of Style*. Notes must be in endnote format and the first reference should include all bibliographical information. No additional bibliography is necessary. For additional references, omit the title of the work and give only the last name of the author followed by a comma and the page number of the reference. When more than one work by the same author has been cited, a shortened title is necessary, in addition to the author's last name. For example:

Notes

1. David Stafford, *Britain and European Resistance, 1940-1945* (Toronto: University of Toronto Press, 1980), 90.

2. James F. Powers, "Frontier Municipal Baths and Social Interaction in Thirteenth-Century Spain," *American Historical Review* 84 (June 1979): 655.

3. Stafford, 89.

4. H.H. Rowley, ed., *The Old Testament and Modern Study* (Oxford: Clarendon Press, 1951), 50.

5. Jaroslav Pelikan et al., *Religion and the University*, York University Invitation Lecture Series (Toronto: University of Toronto Press, 1964), 109.

6. Mark Graubard, trans., and John Parker, ed., *Tidings out of Brazil* (Minneapolis: University of Minnesota Press, 1957), 13.

7. Dorothy Van Ghent, "The Dickens World: A View from Todgers's," in George H. Ford and Lauriat Lane, Jr., eds., *The Dickens Critics* (Ithaca, N.Y.: Cornell University Press, 1961), 213-32.